Ibn Sīnā (Avicenna): A Very Short Introduction

VERY SHORT INTRODUCTIONS are for anyone wanting a stimulating and accessible way into a new subject. They are written by experts, and have been translated into more than 45 different languages.

The series began in 1995, and now covers a wide variety of topics in every discipline. The VSI library currently contains over 700 volumes—a Very Short Introduction to everything from Psychology and Philosophy of Science to American History and Relativity—and continues to grow in every subject area.

Very Short Introductions available now:

ABOLITIONISM Richard S. Newman
THE ABRAHAMIC RELIGIONS Charles L. Cohen
ACCOUNTING Christopher Nobes
ADDICTION Keith Humphreys
ADOLESCENCE Peter K. Smith
THEODOR W. ADORNO Andrew Bowie
ADVERTISING Winston Fletcher
AERIAL WARFARE Frank Ledwidge
AESTHETICS Bence Nanay
AFRICAN AMERICAN HISTORY Jonathan Scott Holloway
AFRICAN AMERICAN RELIGION Eddie S. Glaude Jr
AFRICAN HISTORY John Parker and Richard Rathbone
AFRICAN POLITICS Ian Taylor
AFRICAN RELIGIONS Jacob K. Olupona
AGEING Nancy A. Pachana
AGNOSTICISM Robin Le Poidevin
AGRICULTURE Paul Brassley and Richard Soffe
ALEXANDER THE GREAT Hugh Bowden
ALGEBRA Peter M. Higgins
AMERICAN BUSINESS HISTORY Walter A. Friedman
AMERICAN CULTURAL HISTORY Eric Avila
AMERICAN FOREIGN RELATIONS Andrew Preston
AMERICAN HISTORY Paul S. Boyer
AMERICAN IMMIGRATION David A. Gerber
AMERICAN INTELLECTUAL HISTORY Jennifer Ratner-Rosenhagen
THE AMERICAN JUDICIAL SYSTEM Charles L. Zelden
AMERICAN LEGAL HISTORY G. Edward White
AMERICAN MILITARY HISTORY Joseph T. Glatthaar
AMERICAN NAVAL HISTORY Craig L. Symonds
AMERICAN POETRY David Caplan
AMERICAN POLITICAL HISTORY Donald Critchlow
AMERICAN POLITICAL PARTIES AND ELECTIONS L. Sandy Maisel
AMERICAN POLITICS Richard M. Valelly
THE AMERICAN PRESIDENCY Charles O. Jones
THE AMERICAN REVOLUTION Robert J. Allison
AMERICAN SLAVERY Heather Andrea Williams
THE AMERICAN SOUTH Charles Reagan Wilson
THE AMERICAN WEST Stephen Aron
AMERICAN WOMEN'S HISTORY Susan Ware
AMPHIBIANS T. S. Kemp
ANAESTHESIA Aidan O'Donnell

ANALYTIC PHILOSOPHY Michael Beaney
ANARCHISM Alex Prichard
ANCIENT ASSYRIA Karen Radner
ANCIENT EGYPT Ian Shaw
ANCIENT EGYPTIAN ART AND ARCHITECTURE Christina Riggs
ANCIENT GREECE Paul Cartledge
ANCIENT GREEK AND ROMAN SCIENCE Liba Taub
THE ANCIENT NEAR EAST Amanda H. Podany
ANCIENT PHILOSOPHY Julia Annas
ANCIENT WARFARE Harry Sidebottom
ANGELS David Albert Jones
ANGLICANISM Mark Chapman
THE ANGLO-SAXON AGE John Blair
ANIMAL BEHAVIOUR Tristram D. Wyatt
THE ANIMAL KINGDOM Peter Holland
ANIMAL RIGHTS David DeGrazia
ANSELM Thomas Williams
THE ANTARCTIC Klaus Dodds
ANTHROPOCENE Erle C. Ellis
ANTISEMITISM Steven Beller
ANXIETY Daniel Freeman and Jason Freeman
THE APOCRYPHAL GOSPELS Paul Foster
APPLIED MATHEMATICS Alain Goriely
THOMAS AQUINAS Fergus Kerr
ARBITRATION Thomas Schultz and Thomas Grant
ARCHAEOLOGY Paul Bahn
ARCHITECTURE Andrew Ballantyne
THE ARCTIC Klaus Dodds and Jamie Woodward
HANNAH ARENDT Dana Villa
ARISTOCRACY William Doyle
ARISTOTLE Jonathan Barnes
ART HISTORY Dana Arnold
ART THEORY Cynthia Freeland
ARTIFICIAL INTELLIGENCE Margaret A. Boden
ASIAN AMERICAN HISTORY Madeline Y. Hsu
ASTROBIOLOGY David C. Catling
ASTROPHYSICS James Binney
ATHEISM Julian Baggini
THE ATMOSPHERE Paul I. Palmer
AUGUSTINE Henry Chadwick
JANE AUSTEN Tom Keymer
AUSTRALIA Kenneth Morgan
AUTISM Uta Frith
AUTOBIOGRAPHY Laura Marcus
THE AVANT GARDE David Cottington
THE AZTECS Davíd Carrasco
BABYLONIA Trevor Bryce
BACTERIA Sebastian G. B. Amyes
BANKING John Goddard and John O. S. Wilson
BARTHES Jonathan Culler
THE BEATS David Sterritt
BEAUTY Roger Scruton
LUDWIG VAN BEETHOVEN Mark Evan Bonds
BEHAVIOURAL ECONOMICS Michelle Baddeley
BESTSELLERS John Sutherland
THE BIBLE John Riches
BIBLICAL ARCHAEOLOGY Eric H. Cline
BIG DATA Dawn E. Holmes
BIOCHEMISTRY Mark Lorch
BIOGEOGRAPHY Mark V. Lomolino
BIOGRAPHY Hermione Lee
BIOMETRICS Michael Fairhurst
ELIZABETH BISHOP Jonathan F. S. Post
BLACK HOLES Katherine Blundell
BLASPHEMY Yvonne Sherwood
BLOOD Chris Cooper
THE BLUES Elijah Wald
THE BODY Chris Shilling
THE BOHEMIANS David Weir
NIELS BOHR J. L. Heilbron
THE BOOK OF COMMON PRAYER Brian Cummings
THE BOOK OF MORMON Terryl Givens
BORDERS Alexander C. Diener and Joshua Hagen
THE BRAIN Michael O'Shea
BRANDING Robert Jones
THE BRICS Andrew F. Cooper
BRITISH CINEMA Charles Barr

THE BRITISH CONSTITUTION Martin Loughlin
THE BRITISH EMPIRE Ashley Jackson
BRITISH POLITICS Tony Wright
BUDDHA Michael Carrithers
BUDDHISM Damien Keown
BUDDHIST ETHICS Damien Keown
BYZANTIUM Peter Sarris
CALVINISM Jon Balserak
ALBERT CAMUS Oliver Gloag
CANADA Donald Wright
CANCER Nicholas James
CAPITALISM James Fulcher
CATHOLICISM Gerald O'Collins
CAUSATION Stephen Mumford and Rani Lill Anjum
THE CELL Terence Allen and Graham Cowling
THE CELTS Barry Cunliffe
CHAOS Leonard Smith
GEOFFREY CHAUCER David Wallace
CHEMISTRY Peter Atkins
CHILD PSYCHOLOGY Usha Goswami
CHILDREN'S LITERATURE Kimberley Reynolds
CHINESE LITERATURE Sabina Knight
CHOICE THEORY Michael Allingham
CHRISTIAN ART Beth Williamson
CHRISTIAN ETHICS D. Stephen Long
CHRISTIANITY Linda Woodhead
CIRCADIAN RHYTHMS Russell Foster and Leon Kreitzman
CITIZENSHIP Richard Bellamy
CITY PLANNING Carl Abbott
CIVIL ENGINEERING David Muir Wood
THE CIVIL RIGHTS MOVEMENT Thomas C. Holt
CLASSICAL LITERATURE William Allan
CLASSICAL MYTHOLOGY Helen Morales
CLASSICS Mary Beard and John Henderson
CLAUSEWITZ Michael Howard
CLIMATE Mark Maslin
CLIMATE CHANGE Mark Maslin
CLINICAL PSYCHOLOGY Susan Llewelyn and Katie Aafjes-van Doorn
COGNITIVE BEHAVIOURAL THERAPY Freda McManus
COGNITIVE NEUROSCIENCE Richard Passingham
THE COLD WAR Robert J. McMahon
COLONIAL AMERICA Alan Taylor
COLONIAL LATIN AMERICAN LITERATURE Rolena Adorno
COMBINATORICS Robin Wilson
COMEDY Matthew Bevis
COMMUNISM Leslie Holmes
COMPARATIVE LITERATURE Ben Hutchinson
COMPETITION AND ANTITRUST LAW Ariel Ezrachi
COMPLEXITY John H. Holland
THE COMPUTER Darrel Ince
COMPUTER SCIENCE Subrata Dasgupta
CONCENTRATION CAMPS Dan Stone
CONDENSED MATTER PHYSICS Ross H. McKenzie
CONFUCIANISM Daniel K. Gardner
THE CONQUISTADORS Matthew Restall and Felipe Fernández-Armesto
CONSCIENCE Paul Strohm
CONSCIOUSNESS Susan Blackmore
CONTEMPORARY ART Julian Stallabrass
CONTEMPORARY FICTION Robert Eaglestone
CONTINENTAL PHILOSOPHY Simon Critchley
COPERNICUS Owen Gingerich
CORAL REEFS Charles Sheppard
CORPORATE SOCIAL RESPONSIBILITY Jeremy Moon
CORRUPTION Leslie Holmes
COSMOLOGY Peter Coles
COUNTRY MUSIC Richard Carlin
CREATIVITY Vlad Glăveanu
CRIME FICTION Richard Bradford
CRIMINAL JUSTICE Julian V. Roberts
CRIMINOLOGY Tim Newburn
CRITICAL THEORY Stephen Eric Bronner
THE CRUSADES Christopher Tyerman

CRYPTOGRAPHY Fred Piper and Sean Murphy
CRYSTALLOGRAPHY A. M. Glazer
THE CULTURAL REVOLUTION Richard Curt Kraus
DADA AND SURREALISM David Hopkins
DANTE Peter Hainsworth and David Robey
DARWIN Jonathan Howard
THE DEAD SEA SCROLLS Timothy H. Lim
DECADENCE David Weir
DECOLONIZATION Dane Kennedy
DEMENTIA Kathleen Taylor
DEMOCRACY Naomi Zack
DEMOGRAPHY Sarah Harper
DEPRESSION Jan Scott and Mary Jane Tacchi
DERRIDA Simon Glendinning
DESCARTES Tom Sorell
DESERTS Nick Middleton
DESIGN John Heskett
DEVELOPMENT Ian Goldin
DEVELOPMENTAL BIOLOGY Lewis Wolpert
THE DEVIL Darren Oldridge
DIASPORA Kevin Kenny
CHARLES DICKENS Jenny Hartley
DICTIONARIES Lynda Mugglestone
DINOSAURS David Norman
DIPLOMATIC HISTORY Joseph M. Siracusa
DOCUMENTARY FILM Patricia Aufderheide
DREAMING J. Allan Hobson
DRUGS Les Iversen
DRUIDS Barry Cunliffe
DYNASTY Jeroen Duindam
DYSLEXIA Margaret J. Snowling
EARLY MUSIC Thomas Forrest Kelly
THE EARTH Martin Redfern
EARTH SYSTEM SCIENCE Tim Lenton
ECOLOGY Jaboury Ghazoul
ECONOMICS Partha Dasgupta
EDUCATION Gary Thomas
EGYPTIAN MYTH Geraldine Pinch
EIGHTEENTH-CENTURY BRITAIN Paul Langford
THE ELEMENTS Philip Ball
EMOTION Dylan Evans
EMPIRE Stephen Howe
EMPLOYMENT LAW David Cabrelli
ENERGY SYSTEMS Nick Jenkins
ENGELS Terrell Carver
ENGINEERING David Blockley
THE ENGLISH LANGUAGE Simon Horobin
ENGLISH LITERATURE Jonathan Bate
THE ENLIGHTENMENT John Robertson
ENTREPRENEURSHIP Paul Westhead and Mike Wright
ENVIRONMENTAL ECONOMICS Stephen Smith
ENVIRONMENTAL ETHICS Robin Attfield
ENVIRONMENTAL LAW Elizabeth Fisher
ENVIRONMENTAL POLITICS Andrew Dobson
ENZYMES Paul Engel
EPICUREANISM Catherine Wilson
EPIDEMIOLOGY Rodolfo Saracci
ETHICS Simon Blackburn
ETHNOMUSICOLOGY Timothy Rice
THE ETRUSCANS Christopher Smith
EUGENICS Philippa Levine
THE EUROPEAN UNION Simon Usherwood and John Pinder
EUROPEAN UNION LAW Anthony Arnull
EVANGELICALISM John G. Stackhouse Jr.
EVIL Luke Russell
EVOLUTION Brian and Deborah Charlesworth
EXISTENTIALISM Thomas Flynn
EXPLORATION Stewart A. Weaver
EXTINCTION Paul B. Wignall
THE EYE Michael Land
FAIRY TALE Marina Warner
FAMILY LAW Jonathan Herring
MICHAEL FARADAY Frank A. J. L. James
FASCISM Kevin Passmore
FASHION Rebecca Arnold
FEDERALISM Mark J. Rozell and Clyde Wilcox
FEMINISM Margaret Walters

FILM Michael Wood
FILM MUSIC Kathryn Kalinak
FILM NOIR James Naremore
FIRE Andrew C. Scott
THE FIRST WORLD WAR Michael Howard
FLUID MECHANICS Eric Lauga
FOLK MUSIC Mark Slobin
FOOD John Krebs
FORENSIC PSYCHOLOGY David Canter
FORENSIC SCIENCE Jim Fraser
FORESTS Jaboury Ghazoul
FOSSILS Keith Thomson
FOUCAULT Gary Gutting
THE FOUNDING FATHERS R. B. Bernstein
FRACTALS Kenneth Falconer
FREE SPEECH Nigel Warburton
FREE WILL Thomas Pink
FREEMASONRY Andreas Önnerfors
FRENCH LITERATURE John D. Lyons
FRENCH PHILOSOPHY Stephen Gaukroger and Knox Peden
THE FRENCH REVOLUTION William Doyle
FREUD Anthony Storr
FUNDAMENTALISM Malise Ruthven
FUNGI Nicholas P. Money
THE FUTURE Jennifer M. Gidley
GALAXIES John Gribbin
GALILEO Stillman Drake
GAME THEORY Ken Binmore
GANDHI Bhikhu Parekh
GARDEN HISTORY Gordon Campbell
GENES Jonathan Slack
GENIUS Andrew Robinson
GENOMICS John Archibald
GEOGRAPHY John Matthews and David Herbert
GEOLOGY Jan Zalasiewicz
GEOMETRY Maciej Dunajski
GEOPHYSICS William Lowrie
GEOPOLITICS Klaus Dodds
GERMAN LITERATURE Nicholas Boyle
GERMAN PHILOSOPHY Andrew Bowie
THE GHETTO Bryan Cheyette
GLACIATION David J. A. Evans
GLOBAL CATASTROPHES Bill McGuire
GLOBAL ECONOMIC HISTORY Robert C. Allen
GLOBAL ISLAM Nile Green
GLOBALIZATION Manfred B. Steger
GOD John Bowker
GÖDEL'S THEOREM A. W. Moore
GOETHE Ritchie Robertson
THE GOTHIC Nick Groom
GOVERNANCE Mark Bevir
GRAVITY Timothy Clifton
THE GREAT DEPRESSION AND THE NEW DEAL Eric Rauchway
HABEAS CORPUS Amanda L. Tyler
HABERMAS James Gordon Finlayson
THE HABSBURG EMPIRE Martyn Rady
HAPPINESS Daniel M. Haybron
THE HARLEM RENAISSANCE Cheryl A. Wall
THE HEBREW BIBLE AS LITERATURE Tod Linafelt
HEGEL Peter Singer
HEIDEGGER Michael Inwood
THE HELLENISTIC AGE Peter Thonemann
HEREDITY John Waller
HERMENEUTICS Jens Zimmermann
HERODOTUS Jennifer T. Roberts
HIEROGLYPHS Penelope Wilson
HINDUISM Kim Knott
HISTORY John H. Arnold
THE HISTORY OF ASTRONOMY Michael Hoskin
THE HISTORY OF CHEMISTRY William H. Brock
THE HISTORY OF CHILDHOOD James Marten
THE HISTORY OF CINEMA Geoffrey Nowell-Smith
THE HISTORY OF COMPUTING Doron Swade
THE HISTORY OF EMOTIONS Thomas Dixon
THE HISTORY OF LIFE Michael Benton
THE HISTORY OF MATHEMATICS Jacqueline Stedall
THE HISTORY OF MEDICINE William Bynum

THE HISTORY OF PHYSICS J. L. Heilbron
THE HISTORY OF POLITICAL THOUGHT Richard Whatmore
THE HISTORY OF TIME Leofranc Holford-Strevens
HIV AND AIDS Alan Whiteside
HOBBES Richard Tuck
HOLLYWOOD Peter Decherney
THE HOLY ROMAN EMPIRE Joachim Whaley
HOME Michael Allen Fox
HOMER Barbara Graziosi
HORMONES Martin Luck
HORROR Darryl Jones
HUMAN ANATOMY Leslie Klenerman
HUMAN EVOLUTION Bernard Wood
HUMAN PHYSIOLOGY Jamie A. Davies
HUMAN RESOURCE MANAGEMENT Adrian Wilkinson
HUMAN RIGHTS Andrew Clapham
HUMANISM Stephen Law
HUME James A. Harris
HUMOUR Noël Carroll
IBN SĪNĀ (AVICENNA) Peter Adamson
THE ICE AGE Jamie Woodward
IDENTITY Florian Coulmas
IDEOLOGY Michael Freeden
THE IMMUNE SYSTEM Paul Klenerman
INDIAN CINEMA Ashish Rajadhyaksha
INDIAN PHILOSOPHY Sue Hamilton
THE INDUSTRIAL REVOLUTION Robert C. Allen
INFECTIOUS DISEASE Marta L. Wayne and Benjamin M. Bolker
INFINITY Ian Stewart
INFORMATION Luciano Floridi
INNOVATION Mark Dodgson and David Gann
INTELLECTUAL PROPERTY Siva Vaidhyanathan
INTELLIGENCE Ian J. Deary
INTERNATIONAL LAW Vaughan Lowe
INTERNATIONAL MIGRATION Khalid Koser
INTERNATIONAL RELATIONS Christian Reus-Smit
INTERNATIONAL SECURITY Christopher S. Browning
INSECTS Simon Leather
IRAN Ali M. Ansari
ISLAM Malise Ruthven
ISLAMIC HISTORY Adam Silverstein
ISLAMIC LAW Mashood A. Baderin
ISOTOPES Rob Ellam
ITALIAN LITERATURE Peter Hainsworth and David Robey
HENRY JAMES Susan L. Mizruchi
JAPANESE LITERATURE Alan Tansman
JESUS Richard Bauckham
JEWISH HISTORY David N. Myers
JEWISH LITERATURE Ilan Stavans
JOURNALISM Ian Hargreaves
JAMES JOYCE Colin MacCabe
JUDAISM Norman Solomon
JUNG Anthony Stevens
THE JURY Renée Lettow Lerner
KABBALAH Joseph Dan
KAFKA Ritchie Robertson
KANT Roger Scruton
KEYNES Robert Skidelsky
KIERKEGAARD Patrick Gardiner
KNOWLEDGE Jennifer Nagel
THE KORAN Michael Cook
KOREA Michael J. Seth
LAKES Warwick F. Vincent
LANDSCAPE ARCHITECTURE Ian H. Thompson
LANDSCAPES AND GEOMORPHOLOGY Andrew Goudie and Heather Viles
LANGUAGES Stephen R. Anderson
LATE ANTIQUITY Gillian Clark
LAW Raymond Wacks
THE LAWS OF THERMODYNAMICS Peter Atkins
LEADERSHIP Keith Grint
LEARNING Mark Haselgrove
LEIBNIZ Maria Rosa Antognazza
C. S. LEWIS James Como
LIBERALISM Michael Freeden
LIGHT Ian Walmsley
LINCOLN Allen C. Guelzo
LINGUISTICS Peter Matthews
LITERARY THEORY Jonathan Culler

LOCKE John Dunn
LOGIC Graham Priest
LOVE Ronald de Sousa
MARTIN LUTHER Scott H. Hendrix
MACHIAVELLI Quentin Skinner
MADNESS Andrew Scull
MAGIC Owen Davies
MAGNA CARTA Nicholas Vincent
MAGNETISM Stephen Blundell
MALTHUS Donald Winch
MAMMALS T. S. Kemp
MANAGEMENT John Hendry
NELSON MANDELA Elleke Boehmer
MAO Delia Davin
MARINE BIOLOGY Philip V. Mladenov
MARKETING Kenneth Le Meunier-FitzHugh
THE MARQUIS DE SADE John Phillips
MARTYRDOM Jolyon Mitchell
MARX Peter Singer
MATERIALS Christopher Hall
MATHEMATICAL ANALYSIS Richard Earl
MATHEMATICAL FINANCE Mark H. A. Davis
MATHEMATICS Timothy Gowers
MATTER Geoff Cottrell
THE MAYA Matthew Restall and Amara Solari
THE MEANING OF LIFE Terry Eagleton
MEASUREMENT David Hand
MEDICAL ETHICS Michael Dunn and Tony Hope
MEDICAL LAW Charles Foster
MEDIEVAL BRITAIN John Gillingham and Ralph A. Griffiths
MEDIEVAL LITERATURE Elaine Treharne
MEDIEVAL PHILOSOPHY John Marenbon
MEMORY Jonathan K. Foster
METAPHYSICS Stephen Mumford
METHODISM William J. Abraham
THE MEXICAN REVOLUTION Alan Knight
MICROBIOLOGY Nicholas P. Money
MICROBIOMES Angela E. Douglas
MICROECONOMICS Avinash Dixit
MICROSCOPY Terence Allen
THE MIDDLE AGES Miri Rubin
MILITARY JUSTICE Eugene R. Fidell
MILITARY STRATEGY Antulio J. Echevarria II
JOHN STUART MILL Gregory Claeys
MINERALS David Vaughan
MIRACLES Yujin Nagasawa
MODERN ARCHITECTURE Adam Sharr
MODERN ART David Cottington
MODERN BRAZIL Anthony W. Pereira
MODERN CHINA Rana Mitter
MODERN DRAMA Kirsten E. Shepherd-Barr
MODERN FRANCE Vanessa R. Schwartz
MODERN INDIA Craig Jeffrey
MODERN IRELAND Senia Pašeta
MODERN ITALY Anna Cento Bull
MODERN JAPAN Christopher Goto-Jones
MODERN LATIN AMERICAN LITERATURE Roberto González Echevarría
MODERN WAR Richard English
MODERNISM Christopher Butler
MOLECULAR BIOLOGY Aysha Divan and Janice A. Royds
MOLECULES Philip Ball
MONASTICISM Stephen J. Davis
THE MONGOLS Morris Rossabi
MONTAIGNE William M. Hamlin
MOONS David A. Rothery
MORMONISM Richard Lyman Bushman
MOUNTAINS Martin F. Price
MUHAMMAD Jonathan A. C. Brown
MULTICULTURALISM Ali Rattansi
MULTILINGUALISM John C. Maher
MUSIC Nicholas Cook
MUSIC AND TECHNOLOGY Mark Katz
MYTH Robert A. Segal
NANOTECHNOLOGY Philip Moriarty
NAPOLEON David A. Bell
THE NAPOLEONIC WARS Mike Rapport
NATIONALISM Steven Grosby
NATIVE AMERICAN LITERATURE Sean Teuton

NAVIGATION Jim Bennett
NAZI GERMANY Jane Caplan
NEGOTIATION Carrie Menkel-Meadow
NEOLIBERALISM Manfred B. Steger and Ravi K. Roy
NETWORKS Guido Caldarelli and Michele Catanzaro
THE NEW TESTAMENT Luke Timothy Johnson
THE NEW TESTAMENT AS LITERATURE Kyle Keefer
NEWTON Robert Iliffe
NIETZSCHE Michael Tanner
NINETEENTH-CENTURY BRITAIN Christopher Harvie and H. C. G. Matthew
THE NORMAN CONQUEST George Garnett
NORTH AMERICAN INDIANS Theda Perdue and Michael D. Green
NORTHERN IRELAND Marc Mulholland
NOTHING Frank Close
NUCLEAR PHYSICS Frank Close
NUCLEAR POWER Maxwell Irvine
NUCLEAR WEAPONS Joseph M. Siracusa
NUMBER THEORY Robin Wilson
NUMBERS Peter M. Higgins
NUTRITION David A. Bender
OBJECTIVITY Stephen Gaukroger
OBSERVATIONAL ASTRONOMY Geoff Cottrell
OCEANS Dorrik Stow
THE OLD TESTAMENT Michael D. Coogan
THE ORCHESTRA D. Kern Holoman
ORGANIC CHEMISTRY Graham Patrick
ORGANIZATIONS Mary Jo Hatch
ORGANIZED CRIME Georgios A. Antonopoulos and Georgios Papanicolaou
ORTHODOX CHRISTIANITY A. Edward Siecienski
OVID Llewelyn Morgan
PAGANISM Owen Davies
PAKISTAN Pippa Virdee
THE PALESTINIAN-ISRAELI CONFLICT Martin Bunton
PANDEMICS Christian W. McMillen
PARTICLE PHYSICS Frank Close
PAUL E. P. Sanders
IVAN PAVLOV Daniel P. Todes
PEACE Oliver P. Richmond
PENTECOSTALISM William K. Kay
PERCEPTION Brian Rogers
THE PERIODIC TABLE Eric R. Scerri
PHILOSOPHICAL METHOD Timothy Williamson
PHILOSOPHY Edward Craig
PHILOSOPHY IN THE ISLAMIC WORLD Peter Adamson
PHILOSOPHY OF BIOLOGY Samir Okasha
PHILOSOPHY OF LAW Raymond Wacks
PHILOSOPHY OF MIND Barbara Gail Montero
PHILOSOPHY OF PHYSICS David Wallace
PHILOSOPHY OF SCIENCE Samir Okasha
PHILOSOPHY OF RELIGION Tim Bayne
PHOTOGRAPHY Steve Edwards
PHYSICAL CHEMISTRY Peter Atkins
PHYSICS Sidney Perkowitz
PILGRIMAGE Ian Reader
PLAGUE Paul Slack
PLANETARY SYSTEMS Raymond T. Pierrehumbert
PLANETS David A. Rothery
PLANTS Timothy Walker
PLATE TECTONICS Peter Molnar
PLATO Julia Annas
POETRY Bernard O'Donoghue
POLITICAL PHILOSOPHY David Miller
POLITICS Kenneth Minogue
POLYGAMY Sarah M. S. Pearsall
POPULISM Cas Mudde and Cristóbal Rovira Kaltwasser
POSTCOLONIALISM Robert J. C. Young
POSTMODERNISM Christopher Butler
POSTSTRUCTURALISM Catherine Belsey
POVERTY Philip N. Jefferson
PREHISTORY Chris Gosden

PRESOCRATIC PHILOSOPHY Catherine Osborne
PRIVACY Raymond Wacks
PROBABILITY John Haigh
PROGRESSIVISM Walter Nugent
PROHIBITION W. J. Rorabaugh
PROJECTS Andrew Davies
PROTESTANTISM Mark A. Noll
PSEUDOSCIENCE Michael D. Gordin
PSYCHIATRY Tom Burns
PSYCHOANALYSIS Daniel Pick
PSYCHOLOGY Gillian Butler and Freda McManus
PSYCHOLOGY OF MUSIC Elizabeth Hellmuth Margulis
PSYCHOPATHY Essi Viding
PSYCHOTHERAPY Tom Burns and Eva Burns-Lundgren
PUBLIC ADMINISTRATION Stella Z. Theodoulou and Ravi K. Roy
PUBLIC HEALTH Virginia Berridge
PURITANISM Francis J. Bremer
THE QUAKERS Pink Dandelion
QUANTUM THEORY John Polkinghorne
RACISM Ali Rattansi
RADIOACTIVITY Claudio Tuniz
RASTAFARI Ennis B. Edmonds
READING Belinda Jack
THE REAGAN REVOLUTION Gil Troy
REALITY Jan Westerhoff
RECONSTRUCTION Allen C. Guelzo
THE REFORMATION Peter Marshall
REFUGEES Gil Loescher
RELATIVITY Russell Stannard
RELIGION Thomas A. Tweed
RELIGION IN AMERICA Timothy Beal
THE RENAISSANCE Jerry Brotton
RENAISSANCE ART Geraldine A. Johnson
RENEWABLE ENERGY Nick Jelley
REPTILES T. S. Kemp
REVOLUTIONS Jack A. Goldstone
RHETORIC Richard Toye
RISK Baruch Fischhoff and John Kadvany
RITUAL Barry Stephenson
RIVERS Nick Middleton
ROBOTICS Alan Winfield
ROCKS Jan Zalasiewicz
ROMAN BRITAIN Peter Salway
THE ROMAN EMPIRE Christopher Kelly
THE ROMAN REPUBLIC David M. Gwynn
ROMANTICISM Michael Ferber
ROUSSEAU Robert Wokler
RUSSELL A. C. Grayling
THE RUSSIAN ECONOMY Richard Connolly
RUSSIAN HISTORY Geoffrey Hosking
RUSSIAN LITERATURE Catriona Kelly
THE RUSSIAN REVOLUTION S. A. Smith
SAINTS Simon Yarrow
SAMURAI Michael Wert
SAVANNAS Peter A. Furley
SCEPTICISM Duncan Pritchard
SCHIZOPHRENIA Chris Frith and Eve Johnstone
SCHOPENHAUER Christopher Janaway
SCIENCE AND RELIGION Thomas Dixon and Adam R. Shapiro
SCIENCE FICTION David Seed
THE SCIENTIFIC REVOLUTION Lawrence M. Principe
SCOTLAND Rab Houston
SECULARISM Andrew Copson
SEXUAL SELECTION Marlene Zuk and Leigh W. Simmons
SEXUALITY Véronique Mottier
WILLIAM SHAKESPEARE Stanley Wells
SHAKESPEARE'S COMEDIES Bart van Es
SHAKESPEARE'S SONNETS AND POEMS Jonathan F. S. Post
SHAKESPEARE'S TRAGEDIES Stanley Wells
GEORGE BERNARD SHAW Christopher Wixson
MARY SHELLEY Charlotte Gordon
THE SHORT STORY Andrew Kahn
SIKHISM Eleanor Nesbitt
SILENT FILM Donna Kornhaber
THE SILK ROAD James A. Millward
SLANG Jonathon Green
SLEEP Steven W. Lockley and Russell G. Foster
SMELL Matthew Cobb

ADAM SMITH Christopher J. Berry
SOCIAL AND CULTURAL ANTHROPOLOGY John Monaghan and Peter Just
SOCIAL PSYCHOLOGY Richard J. Crisp
SOCIAL WORK Sally Holland and Jonathan Scourfield
SOCIALISM Michael Newman
SOCIOLINGUISTICS John Edwards
SOCIOLOGY Steve Bruce
SOCRATES C. C. W. Taylor
SOFT MATTER Tom McLeish
SOUND Mike Goldsmith
SOUTHEAST ASIA James R. Rush
THE SOVIET UNION Stephen Lovell
THE SPANISH CIVIL WAR Helen Graham
SPANISH LITERATURE Jo Labanyi
THE SPARTANS Andrew J. Bayliss
SPINOZA Roger Scruton
SPIRITUALITY Philip Sheldrake
SPORT Mike Cronin
STARS Andrew King
STATISTICS David J. Hand
STEM CELLS Jonathan Slack
STOICISM Brad Inwood
STRUCTURAL ENGINEERING David Blockley
STUART BRITAIN John Morrill
SUBURBS Carl Abbott
THE SUN Philip Judge
SUPERCONDUCTIVITY Stephen Blundell
SUPERSTITION Stuart Vyse
SYMMETRY Ian Stewart
SYNAESTHESIA Julia Simner
SYNTHETIC BIOLOGY Jamie A. Davies
SYSTEMS BIOLOGY Eberhard O. Voit
TAXATION Stephen Smith
TEETH Peter S. Ungar
TERRORISM Charles Townshend
THEATRE Marvin Carlson
THEOLOGY David F. Ford
THINKING AND REASONING Jonathan St B. T. Evans
THOUGHT Tim Bayne
TIBETAN BUDDHISM Matthew T. Kapstein
TIDES David George Bowers and Emyr Martyn Roberts
TIME Jenann Ismael
TOCQUEVILLE Harvey C. Mansfield
LEO TOLSTOY Liza Knapp
TOPOLOGY Richard Earl
TRAGEDY Adrian Poole
TRANSLATION Matthew Reynolds
THE TREATY OF VERSAILLES Michael S. Neiberg
TRIGONOMETRY Glen Van Brummelen
THE TROJAN WAR Eric H. Cline
TRUST Katherine Hawley
THE TUDORS John Guy
TWENTIETH-CENTURY BRITAIN Kenneth O. Morgan
TYPOGRAPHY Paul Luna
THE UNITED NATIONS Jussi M. Hanhimäki
UNIVERSITIES AND COLLEGES David Palfreyman and Paul Temple
THE U.S. CIVIL WAR Louis P. Masur
THE U.S. CONGRESS Donald A. Ritchie
THE U.S. CONSTITUTION David J. Bodenhamer
THE U.S. SUPREME COURT Linda Greenhouse
UTILITARIANISM Katarzyna de Lazari-Radek and Peter Singer
UTOPIANISM Lyman Tower Sargent
VATICAN II Shaun Blanchard and Stephen Bullivant
VETERINARY SCIENCE James Yeates
THE VIKINGS Julian D. Richards
VIOLENCE Philip Dwyer
THE VIRGIN MARY Mary Joan Winn Leith
THE VIRTUES Craig A. Boyd and Kevin Timpe
VIRUSES Dorothy H. Crawford
VOLCANOES Michael J. Branney and Jan Zalasiewicz
VOLTAIRE Nicholas Cronk
WAR AND RELIGION Jolyon Mitchell and Joshua Rey
WAR AND TECHNOLOGY Alex Roland
WATER John Finney
WAVES Mike Goldsmith
WEATHER Storm Dunlop

THE WELFARE STATE David Garland
WITCHCRAFT Malcolm Gaskill
WITTGENSTEIN A. C. Grayling
WORK Stephen Fineman
WORLD MUSIC Philip Bohlman
WORLD MYTHOLOGY David Leeming
THE WORLD TRADE ORGANIZATION Amrita Narlikar
WORLD WAR II Gerhard L. Weinberg
WRITING AND SCRIPT Andrew Robinson
ZIONISM Michael Stanislawski
ÉMILE ZOLA Brian Nelson

Available soon:

IMAGINATION Jennifer Gosetti-Ferencei
BIODIVERSITY CONSERVATION David Macdonald
THE VICTORIANS Martin Hewitt

For more information visit our website

www.oup.com/vsi/

Peter Adamson

IBN SĪNĀ (AVICENNA)

A Very Short Introduction

OXFORD
UNIVERSITY PRESS

Great Clarendon Street, Oxford, OX2 6DP,
United Kingdom

Oxford University Press is a department of the University of Oxford.
It furthers the University's objective of excellence in research, scholarship,
and education by publishing worldwide. Oxford is a registered trade mark of
Oxford University Press in the UK and in certain other countries

Published in the United States of America by Oxford University Press
198 Madison Avenue, New York, NY 10016, United States of America

British Library Cataloguing in Publication Data
Data available

Library of Congress Control Number: 2022952225

ISBN 978-0-19-284698-3

Printed and bound by
CPI Group (UK) Ltd, Croydon, CR0 4YY

Contents

Preface

Abū ʿAlī al-Ḥusayn ibn ʿAbdallāh Ibn Sīnā, often called 'Avicenna' in English because this was his name in medieval Latin, was the most important and influential philosopher of the Islamic world. His impact on Islamic intellectual culture can be compared to that of Plato and Aristotle in classical antiquity, or Kant in modern European philosophy, in that all subsequent thinkers had to respond to him favourably or unfavourably, explicitly or implicitly, directly or indirectly. He supplanted Aristotle as the figure who, more than any other, represented what 'philosophy' (*falsafa*) was. We can see this from a backhanded compliment paid by his most famous critic: when the theologian al-Ghazālī (d. 1111) wrote a refutation of Ibn Sīnā, he called it simply *Incoherence of the Philosophers* (*Tahāfut al-falāsifa*). To criticize Ibn Sīnā was, it seems, to criticize philosophy itself.

Actually things are a bit more complicated than that, because the word *falsafa* evoked in al-Ghazālī's title meant something narrower than our term 'philosophy'. To be a *faylasūf*, that is, a practitioner of *falsafa*, was to uphold certain doctrines associated specifically with Ibn Sīnā, such as the necessity and eternity of the world, an understanding of God as a pure intellect who does not grasp anything but universal truths, and a conception of science as the exploration of essential natures and necessary causal connections. Al-Ghazālī rejected all this. But he was a philosopher in his own way, whose own ideas were shaped by the tradition of rationalist Islamic theology or *kalām*. I mention this because one theme we'll be pursuing in this book is the relation between Ibn Sīnā and *kalām*. We'll find that later thinkers in the Islamic world often saw philosophy in a more general sense (they called it *ḥikma*, literally 'wisdom') as a kind of contest between Ibn Sīnā's *falsafa* and traditional *kalām*. In some cases they saw Ibn Sīnā as adopting a certain position within pre-existing *kalām* debates, as on the status of the non-existent or the nature of good and evil.

We'll get into all that in Chapter 6, when we turn to discuss his legacy. I will not tell the full story of his reception there, as that would mean charting the whole history of philosophy in the Islamic world from his death in the 11th century until today. Nor will I be able to give a thorough portrait of philosophy in the time before Ibn Sīnā, though I will sketch this in Chapter 1. For the broad contours of philosophy before and after Ibn Sīnā, the reader may instead be referred to my earlier volume in this same series, *A Very Short Introduction to Philosophy in the Islamic World.*

An incredible but true fact about Ibn Sīnā is that his place in the history of philosophy is matched by his place in the history of medicine. Actually, if you asked an intellectual of the European Renaissance what 'Avicenna' was most famous for, you'd probably be referred not to his metaphysics or theory of the soul, though these aspects of his achievement were certainly still known in Latin Christendom at that time. Instead, they would mention his *Canon of Medicine* (*Qānūn fī l-ṭibb*), a tremendously successful attempt to distil the teachings of ancient and previous Islamic medicine into a single, well-organized reference work. I will duly be touching on his contributions in medicine, and paying special attention to his theory of science, since that is the point where his philosophical and scientific endeavours intersected.

Indeed, understanding Ibn Sīnā requires grasping the interconnections between the different areas of his thought.

He was a profoundly systematic philosopher, who experimented with different ways of leading readers into and through his system. His writings are often difficult, in part for this reason. But this book is designed to prepare you for delving deeper into those writings, many of which are available in English, and into the vast and impressive modern scholarship on his thought (for recommendations where to start, see the end of this volume). We live in a time when non-European philosophy is of interest to a growing audience, and certainly Ibn Sīnā is among the most significant non-European philosophers. At the same time, those who are acquainted with the history of ancient and medieval philosophy in Europe will discover many connections with Ibn Sīnā. Though he was self-consciously innovative and independently minded, practically every page of his writings responds to the Greek philosophical legacy, especially Aristotle, and as already mentioned his relevance to later philosophy in Europe was enormous. So whether you are trying to move past Eurocentric narratives of the history of philosophy, or to gain a better understanding of European ideas and their reception, Ibn Sīnā is the philosopher for you.

List of illustrations

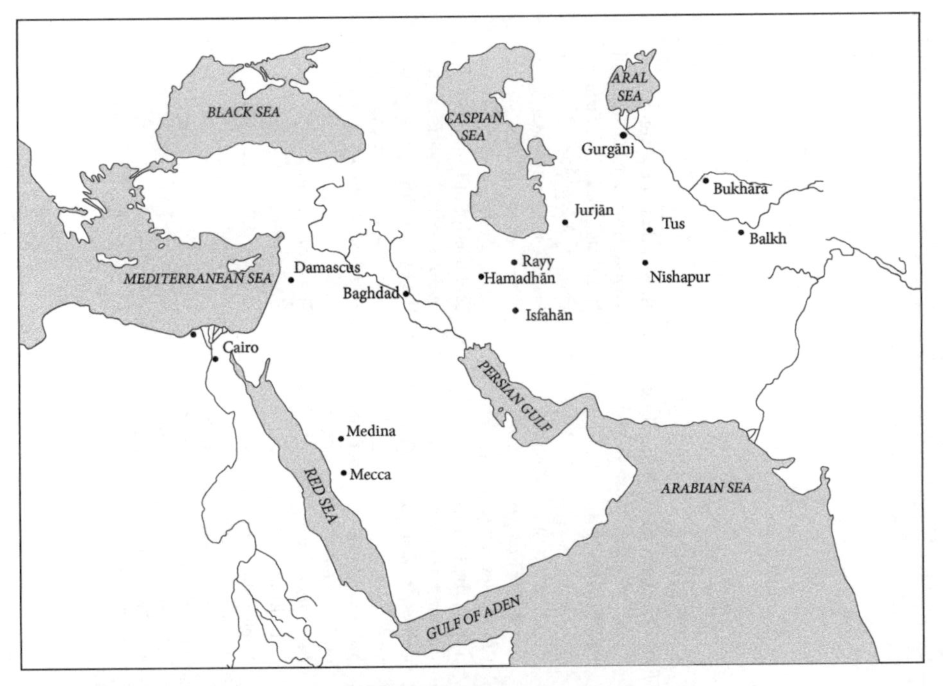

The Islamic East, indicating cities including those visited by Ibn Sīnā.

Chapter 1
Life and works

We know more about Ibn Sīnā's life than we could have any reason to expect, thanks to the survival of his autobiography. It tells the story of a brilliant man who knew full well just how brilliant he was, and therefore offered himself as a model to be imitated by others who wanted to devote their lives to knowledge. It also tells the story of a man who confronted many practical obstacles, from ransacked saddlebags to imprisonment, as he journeyed far and wide in search of the patronage that he needed to be a peacefully established scholar. He did find quite a few patrons, but precious little peace.

Ibn Sīnā and his predecessors

The conditions for Ibn Sīnā's intellectual project were created above all by the Arabic translation movement, which unfolded from the late 8th to the mid-10th century. In this massive undertaking, many works of Greek science and philosophy were rendered into Arabic, with the financial support of the elite of Muslim society. Sometimes translators worked directly from Greek manuscripts, sometimes from Syriac intermediary versions. In fact philosophy, especially but not exclusively Aristotle's logical writings, had already been pursued for centuries by scholars writing in the Syriac language. This means that there was no gap in the transmission of Greek thought from late antiquity to the

Islamic context. Rather, through the Syriac tradition there was continuity from the time of the school of commentators on Aristotle at the Egyptian city of Alexandria, in the 5th and 6th centuries, right up to the 9th century, during the 'Abbāsid caliphate. This was the time of al-Kindī (d. after 870), an intimate of the caliphal family who is usually acknowledged as the first Muslim philosopher. He oversaw the work of translators rendering philosophical and scientific works into Arabic. For this task al-Kindī and his patrons turned to Christian scholars because they were able to work with the Greek or Syriac base texts.

I mention this not only to give credit where it is due, but to get across an important point about philosophy, or rather *falsafa*, in this early period: it was seen as a foreign import, one strongly associated with the Christians who were responsible for importing it. In the period before Ibn Sīnā, *falsafa* did not mean just any engagement with what we would now call 'philosophical' topics, but engagement with the fruits of the Greek–Syriac–Arabic translation movement (including mathematics and the sciences). Many *falāsifa* were themselves Christians, some being both translators and authors of their own philosophical works. Which is not to say that there were no Muslim philosophers before Ibn Sīnā. Apart from al-Kindī, important early figures included Abū Bakr al-Rāzī (d. 925) and al-Fārābī (d. 950).

But al-Fārābī is the exception that proves the rule. He studied with Christian masters and was involved with the so-called Baghdad school of Aristotelians at Baghdad, all of whom were Christians apart from al-Fārābī himself. Nor was Christianity incidental to their intellectual project. A central figure of the school, Yaḥyā Ibn 'Adī (d. 974), wrote works on Christology and the Trinity, while the last member of the school, Ibn al-Ṭayyib (d. 1043), commented on the Bible. Some sense of the perceived link between Christianity and *falsafa* can be had from the record of a debate between Abū Bishr Mattā (d. 940), founder of the

Abū Bakr al-Rāzī and Galenism

Ibn Sīnā did not have a high opinion of his predecessor Abū Bakr al-Rāzī. He dismissed his philosophical ideas, saying that he 'bit off more than he could chew in his attempts to deal with theology, and even exceeded his abilities when lancing abscesses and examining urine and feces'. But if al-Fārābī was the predecessor from whom Ibn Sīnā took the most doctrinally, al-Rāzī is the closest comparison in matters of self-presentation and authorial persona. Most obviously, he was likewise both physician and philosopher, though in his case medicine was the more important occupation. No thinker of the Islamic world had a greater legacy in medicine, apart from Ibn Sīnā himself; and in the Latin world, medieval and Renaissance readers would turn to 'Rhazes' as an important authority in this field. Both men drew extensively on the great ancient doctor Galen for their medical theories (see Chapter 4). They also took their cue from Galen when it came to intellectual self-presentation. In a way that confounds our expectations of medieval thinkers, al-Rāzī and Ibn Sīnā were self-consciously original and open in criticizing even their most admired predecessors. This is an attitude they learned from Galen. Al-Rāzī applied it to Galen himself in a work bearing the frank title *Doubts About Galen* (*Shukūk 'alā Jālīnūs*). Perhaps Ibn Sīnā was so abusive towards al-Rāzī precisely because he recognized in him a kindred spirit. Ibn Sīnā didn't appreciate competition, even from rivals who were already dead.

(Note that Abū Bakr al-Rāzī is not to be confused with the later Fakhr al-Dīn al-Rāzī, who is mentioned numerous times in this book. 'Al-Rāzī' indicates simply that both hailed from the Persian town of Rayy, which, as it happens, was one of the many cities visited by Ibn Sīnā in his life.)

Baghdad school, and a grammarian named al-Sīrāfī (d. 979). Al-Sīrāfī argued that Arabic grammar, not Greek logic, sets the standard for correct speech. In his diatribe he pointedly made fun of Abū Bishr's religious beliefs: the study of logic had not prevented Abū Bishr from thinking that God could be both one and three!

All this changed when *falsafa* became indelibly linked with Ibn Sīnā. It was thanks to him that *falsafa* entered the intellectual mainstream, rather than being a niche topic pursued by specialists. He successfully completed a project already begun by al-Kindī and al-Fārābī, by showing how the resources of Aristotelian philosophy could be brought to bear on the concerns of the Islamic intelligentsia. Nothing typifies this change more than logic. About a century before Ibn Sīnā, al-Sīrāfī mocked it as a pretentious waste of time. Fast forward to a few generations after Ibn Sīnā, and we find his most famous critic al-Ghazālī mocking those who *denied* the value of logic. It would duly become a standard part of the educational curriculum for religious scholars. In fact textbooks working broadly within the framework of Ibn Sīnā's logic would still be used at universities around the Islamic world in the 20th century.

If Ibn Sīnā was a major factor in the absorption of *falsafa* into mainstream intellectual life, he also helped to decide which aspects of *falsafa* would carry on and which would die out. When modern scholars identify al-Fārābī as the most significant Muslim philosopher before Ibn Sīnā, they are just following Ibn Sīnā's own judgement. He claimed to be unimpressed by the Christian members of the Baghdad school, though research is increasingly showing that he took more from them than he cared to admit. Al-Fārābī was the one Baghdad Aristotelian who won his explicit approval ('all but the most excellent of my predecessors', leaving room for Aristotle at the top). The autobiography tells of Ibn Sīnā's struggles to understand Aristotle's *Metaphysics* until he read a book by al-Fārābī, which finally unveiled its purpose to him. It has been suggested that the insight Ibn Sīnā took from al-Fārābī was that metaphysics is primarily a study of being and not an inquiry into God, as al-Kindī had stated in his most important work, *On First Philosophy*.

Indeed, Ibn Sīnā was arguably responsible for putting an end to what can be called the 'Kindian tradition', simply by ignoring it. I use this phrase to refer to a loosely affiliated group of Muslim thinkers who followed al-Kindī's lead by adopting a rather eclectic approach to the Greek philosophical legacy, which was not constrained by the Aristotelian theory of science. As we'll see, that theory was crucial for Ibn Sīnā, and before him it had been crucial for al-Fārābī. Both of them put great emphasis on the internal structure of each science and the way that the disciplines form a hierarchy, with the lower ones taking their principles from higher ones. By contrast, thinkers of the Kindian tradition tended to pursue intellectual disciplines independently from one another, and were happy to spend time on topics lying altogether outside the Aristotelian curriculum, like the religious sciences, comparative religion, geography, and the practical arts (al-Kindī himself wrote about swords and removing stains from clothes).

The Kindian tradition was also characterized by its heavy use of the late ancient thinkers Plotinus and Proclus—central figures in 'Neoplatonism', a tradition which fuses Plato's thought with ideas taken from Aristotle and the Stoics—who had been translated in al-Kindī's circle. We can see this in a rough contemporary of Ibn Sīnā named Miskawayh, perhaps the last figure we can include in the Kindian tradition. His philosophy was strongly characterized by Neoplatonism, and he quoted more than once from al-Kindī. By contrast Ibn Sīnā showed no interest in al-Kindī, and though he took important ideas from the Neoplatonists, he did so in a tacit and selective manner. In fact he commented on the Arabic version of Plotinus, adopting a rather standoffish attitude towards its doctrine on the soul. It is telling that his most important debt to the Neoplatonic tradition, the idea that the universe emanates necessarily and eternally from God, can already be found in al-Fārābī. Like him, Ibn Sīnā engaged seriously with commentaries on Aristotle that were produced in the aforementioned school at Alexandria, and later rendered into Arabic. These, not Plotinus and Proclus, were the most important late ancient philosophical works for al-Fārābī and Ibn Sīnā, for the simple reason that Aristotle was in their eyes by far the most important ancient philosopher.

It would be inaccurate, though, to see Ibn Sīnā's intellectual context solely in terms of Greek philosophy and its Arabic reception. He did not devote great energy to the Islamic religious sciences, but he was trained as a jurist and produced Quranic commentary. Above all, he was well acquainted with the tradition of *kalām*, or rational Islamic theology. *Kalām* dealt with many central philosophical issues, such as atomism, the nature of good and evil, the conditions for moral responsibility, free will and determinism, and proofs for God's existence. Ibn Sīnā had things to say about all these topics. As we'll see, that often involved responding implicitly to *kalām* debates.

The theologians (*mutakallimūn*) up to his time are usually grouped into two schools, albeit with sub-groups within each school. On the one hand there were the Muʿtazilites, on the other the Ashʿarites, whose name comes from a theologian named al-Ashʿarī (d. 935) who turned against the Muʿtazilite doctrines in which he had been trained. The Muʿtazilites insisted on freedom of the human will, and adopted a rigorous stance on divine simplicity. By contrast al-Ashʿarī and his followers tended towards determinism—they said that God creates the actions performed by humans, who through 'acquisition' (*kasb* or *iktisāb*) become responsible for these actions—and accepted a multiplicity of divine attributes. But some views were common to both schools, notably an account of created substances as atoms ('parts of bodies, which have no further parts') upon which God bestows accidental properties, like motion, rest, and combination of the atoms into complex bodies. The theologians also shared a style of argument, which involved arguing for their own views mostly through the refutation of alternative positions.

For Ibn Sīnā, this was a weakness in *kalām*. Echoing a critique already levelled by al-Fārābī, he deemed the theologians' methods to fall short of proper philosophical demonstration, and to rise only to the level of what Aristotle called 'dialectic'. So on two counts the theologians were in Ibn Sīna's eyes not really 'philosophers'. First, they weren't engaging with Greek sources like Aristotle, that is, weren't doing *falsafa*. Second, they weren't giving the kind of proofs a real philosopher should. But this did not prevent them from being among his most significant sparring partners, on a range of philosophical issues and especially in metaphysics.

Ibn Sīnā and his patrons

Ibn Sīnā lived in a time marked by political conflict, as regional powers competed for territory across greater Persia. This forced him into a career that was peripatetic in every sense of the word: he reinvented Aristotelianism while travelling widely, with longer stays in such cities as Bukhārā, Jurjānj, Rayy, Hamadhān, and Iṣfahān. He was born in the village of Afsana near Bukhārā. The traditional date of his birth, 980 CE, seems to be somewhat too late, and he probably lived into his mid-sixties before dying in 1037 CE (428 of the Islamic calendar). Across these decades he received patronage from a number of rulers, who represent a cross-section of rulers active in this period of Islamic history. It was a time of political instability and fragmentation, subsequent to the effective end of the 'Abbāsid caliphate back in 945. In that year, a family called the Būyids took power in Baghdad and installed a puppet caliph.

1. An image from a historical work, *The Compendium of Chronicles*, depicting warfare during the lifetime of Ibn Sīnā.

The Būyids' rivals to the east were the Sāmānids, who took power in the Persian provinces of the collapsed ʿAbbāsid empire. This is directly relevant to Ibn Sīnā's life story, because his first patron Nūḥ ibn Manṣūr was a Sāmānid. A precocious Ibn Sīnā, only 18 at the time, won a place at Ibn Manṣūr's court by healing him from a disease. When the Sāmānid state was toppled in 999, Ibn Sīnā moved to Jurjān, where he spent about a decade in the service of its ruler ʿAlī Ibn Ma'mūn, receiving special support from one of the latter's ministers. He was again forced to move on, to avoid being drafted into the service of Maḥmūd of Ghazna, who is noted for expanding the reach of Islam into India. Maḥmūd was the patron of al-Bīrūnī (d. *c.*1050), perhaps the only intellectual of the time comparable to Ibn Sīnā himself. Aside from his achievements in science, especially astronomy, al-Bīrūnī took advantage of Maḥmūd's incursions into northern India to learn about the cultures there, and on that basis wrote a massive work comparing Indian intellectual currents (including philosophy) to those of Islam and ancient Greece. We have an exchange of letters between Ibn Sīnā and al-Bīrūnī, in which the former answers the latter's queries about Aristotelian philosophy.

After long travels, Ibn Sīnā wound up in the service of Būyids. First he was at Rayy as a client of the Sayyida ('queen mother'), who held the real power as mother of the nominal ruler Majd al-Dawla. Again it was Ibn Sīnā's medical expertise that got him this job. He left to go to Hamadhān, where he joined the court of Majd al-Dawla's brother Shams al-Dawla. Upon the latter's death in 1021, Ibn Sīnā intrigued to join a renegade governor who had turned against the Būyids, named 'Alā' al-Dawla. Ibn Sīnā was placed under house arrest after this was discovered, but once 'Alā' al-Dawla defeated Shams al-Dawla's son, he was able to join his new patron. He would spend the last seven years of his life in his service. Patronage was thus an important, perhaps even the decisive, factor in Ibn Sīnā's career. It helps to explain the significant attention he devoted to medicine: being a philosophical genius is nice, but it doesn't always pay the bills. He also offered expertise as an administrator, as when he acted as the Sayyida's 'business manager'. Several of his works were written for patrons, notably the one treatise he wrote in his native language of Persian: the *Danesh Nameh* (*Book of Knowledge*), composed for 'Alā' al-Dawla.

The (auto-)biography

Much of the information just surveyed comes from Ibn Sīnā's autobiography and the supplementary material added to it by his student al-Jūzjānī after Ibn Sīnā's death. The resulting document is of course to be taken with a small heap of salt. While it does relay useful factual information, this was not the main goal of either author. Ibn Sīnā sought above all to give a context for understanding his own writings, by explaining his own education, the occasions that led him to write several of his works, and his philosophical methodology. Al-Jūzjānī, meanwhile, was concerned to highlight his own role in Ibn Sīnā's career—notably, he recounts how he prompted the writing of the most famous of Ibn Sīnā's works, *The Healing* (*al-Shifā'*)—and of course to extol his master's prodigious talents.

Along the way we get a good sense of Ibn Sīnā's personality. He was a proud man, not apt to suffer fools, but deeply engaged with his circle of associates and students. In the 'not suffering fools' category, a memorable story related by al-Jūzjānī tells of how Ibn Sīnā prepared an elaborate humiliation for a man who slighted his knowledge of the Arabic language. He produced a fake collection of letters in the style of famous literary figures, which he had supposedly discovered 'while hunting in the desert'. When the impertinent rival was unable to understand the text, Ibn Sīnā was then able to spring his trap by explaining it all masterfully—which of course was an easy task, since he had in fact written the letters himself! The hapless victim of this joke is only one of several intellectual inferiors encountered by our hero. In the autobiographical section Ibn Sīnā recalls how a man named al-Nātilī tried to teach him logic and mathematics, only to be stunned by the superior intelligence of his precocious student. Far more hostile was the mature Ibn Sīnā's attitude towards Abū l-Qāsim al-Kirmānī, a rival philosopher mentioned in passing by al-Jūzjānī. Al-Kirmānī was a fellow client of Ibn Sīnā's patron the Sayyida, and their feud may explain why he left her service to join Shams al-Dawla. So intense was Ibn Sīnā's enmity for al-Kirmānī that he descended to obscene name-calling ('dung-beetle', 'shit-eater').

Which seems a good moment to mention the two most provocative details of the biography: Ibn Sīnā's wine-drinking and sexual prowess. He tells us about the wine himself, in the context of explaining his working methods. As the biography conveys, he was a tremendously industrious scholar, and would often work by lamplight, late into the night. To keep himself awake he would drink wine, which may seem a rather jarring admission in the context of an Islamic society. As for sex, al-Jūzjānī is keen to tell us how 'vigorous' was his master in this appetite, and a few pages later he (apparently) connects this to Ibn Sīnā's death. He was suffering from 'colic' (*qawlanj*), meaning an intestinal obstruction caused by gallstones or kidney stones. This was exacerbated by a combination of factors, including a slave who deliberately overdosed him with opium to avoid detection for theft, and Ibn Sīnā's unwillingness to stop indulging in deleterious sexual intercourse. Fortunately for his reputation, and unfortunately for the entertainment value of the biography, the truth of these matters turns out to be far less outrageous. The drinking can be understood within the context of Galenic medicine, which recognized wine as a fortifying drink due to its supposed heating properties. Wine was also important in Persian culture and tolerated by some Islamic legal schools. As for the sex, it was convincingly argued a few years ago that the reference to fatal overindulgence in intercourse is a later addition to the text, presumably introduced by someone hostile to the great philosopher.

Even without this salacious detail, the biography makes it clear that Ibn Sīnā had anything but a sedate life. He skimped on sleep but apart from that spurned asceticism, something he wittily explained to al-Jūzjānī: 'God the exalted has given me powers in abundance, both inside and out, so I give fully to every power what it has coming to it.' In proof of his abundant 'inside' powers, Ibn Sīnā presents himself in the autobiography largely as an autodidact. Early on he mastered the Quran, jurisprudence, and mathematics, the latter being the occasion for his besting of the would-be teacher al-Nātilī. When he was still a child he encountered partisans of a form of Shiite Islam called Ismāʿīlism, which captured the interest of Ibn Sīnā's father and brother. But our protagonist rejected their teachings ('my soul would not accept it'). It has been suggested that Ibn Sīnā emphasized this in the autobiography in order to underscore his own independent approach to religion and philosophy. This made it impossible for him to accept Ismāʿīlism, given its reliance on the authoritative teachings of an inspired Imam. In his teenaged years Ibn Sīnā mastered medicine, 'not one of the difficult sciences', and then plunged into philosophy, working through the curriculum starting from logic and culminating with metaphysics. It was at this point that al-Fārābī's guide to Aristotle's *Metaphysics* came to his rescue.

Many an eyebrow has been raised by Ibn Sīnā's declaration, towards the end of the autobiography, that at the age of 18 he had reached full maturity as a thinker: 'everything that I knew at that time, is as I know it now; I have not added anything to it, to this day.' This looks like a self-undermining boast—is it really impressive if your philosophical thinking stops developing once you've left puberty? But we should take care to understand the remark in light of the Aristotelian theory of science which is a leitmotif throughout the autobiography. Ibn Sīnā has already explained how he undertook 'verification' of scientific theses by finding syllogisms in support of them. He even kept a kind of file collection for the individual arguments, as we might do today using flash cards. Such demonstrative syllogisms *should* be complete once carefully verified, since they can be put together into unbroken chains of inference that go back to certain first principles, and thus leave no room for doubt or omission. That would still allow plenty of room for shifts in emphasis, different modes of presentation and pedagogical strategy, responses to objections, and so on. And in these respects, we do find wide variation in Ibn Sīnā's corpus.

Ibn Sīnā's works

The story of that corpus evokes a time when books were unique, handwritten objects. He tells in the autobiography of how he was given access to the library at Bukhārā by his first patron, Nuḥ ibn al-Manṣūr. Here he marvelled at the collection of works on offer; tellingly he requested to look particularly at 'books of the ancients', and was able to consult texts he would never manage to see again. When it came to his own books, al-Jūzjānī admits that Ibn Sīnā was liberal in his attitude, not to say cavalier, often handing them to others without keeping a copy for himself. The most hair-raising episode came when Ibn Sīnā's bags were ransacked by soldiers outside Iṣfahān in 1030, resulting in the loss of the *Fair Judgement* (*al-Inṣāf*). But there were other cases in which he had to rewrite texts that had gone missing, which gives al-Jūzjānī the opportunity to boast implausibly about Ibn Sīnā's prodigious feats of memory.

The upshot is a rather chaotic body of work, a situation that becomes still more problematic given the later temptation to ascribe spurious texts to this famous name. Both the authentic and the inauthentic corpora are forbiddingly large. An authoritative list counts about 100 genuine works and dozens of pseudographies; and here it should be borne in mind that some of the genuine 'works' are in fact many short works taken together under a single heading, for instance about 20 homilies and comments on passages from the Quran. The many genuine writings of Ibn Sīnā that survive to the present day show an impressive variety in length, level of difficulty, and genre. These differences reflect above all two issues that faced Ibn Sīnā as an author. What was the most effective way to present his ideas to students and readers? And what stance should he adopt relative to Aristotle's philosophy?

In fact these two issues were connected, since we know that his readers expressed interest in Ibn Sīnā's opinions about the ideas that had come down to their time through the Aristotelian tradition. This applies to *The Healing*, a work that covers all the departments of philosophy as well as disciplines we don't consider to be philosophical nowadays, like mathematics. It is an enormous production with separate books on the various disciplines, with the whole Arabic edition filling a decent-sized shelf. Amazingly, this *magnum opus* was written during the most turbulent time of Ibn Sīnā's life, when he passed from the service of the Būyids to that of 'Alā' al-Dawla.

In his contribution to the biography, al-Jūzjānī tells us that it was he who personally requested a commentary on Aristotle's works from the master, only to be told that Ibn Sīnā preferred to set down his own views. Supposedly, some of this was done from memory without consulting books, owing to the disruption in Ibn

Sīnā's situation. But as his original response to al-Jūzjānī's request shows, this was always intended to be an original and opinionated work, one not bound by the strictures of commentary on Aristotle or anyone else. Indeed, this is a striking feature of Ibn Sīnā's output. Unlike his admired predecessor al-Fārābī and the later Ibn Rushd (Averroes, d. 1198), Ibn Sīnā had no intention of being just a faithful follower of Aristotle, and wrote no commentaries on his works. Instead, *The Healing* covers the topics addressed by Aristotle and more besides, but tackles these in a novel sequence and lays out clearly original positions in what amounts to an (ultimately successful) attempt to replace Aristotle, rather than interpret him.

The closest he came to straightforward exegesis on Aristotle is a work that comes down to us only partially, called *The Fair Judgement* (*al-Inṣāf*); as already mentioned, the full version was lost when his baggage was ransacked. As the name implies, it undertook to pass judgement on earlier philosophical texts, especially Aristotle, but also the Arabic version of Plotinus known as the *Theology of Aristotle*; Ibn Sīnā doubted the authenticity of its ascription to Aristotle but chose to discuss it nonetheless. He is at times remarkably critical, for instance when it comes to Aristotle's attempt to prove God as a mere cause of motion, instead of a cause of existence. Another mostly lost work, called *The Easterners* (*al-Mashriqiyyūn*), would have expressed similar attitudes. The title seems to refer to Ibn Sīnā's personal views as opposed to those of the 'Westerners', that is, the more faithful Aristotelians of the Baghdad School. Ibn Sīnā also composed short refutations aimed against that group, a polemic inspired by his clash with al-Kirmānī.

Aside from *The Healing*, we have several other works that range over the gamut of philosophical disciplines, including the aforementioned Persian text, the *Book of Knowledge*. Another example is *The Salvation* (*al-Najāt*), written in response to a

2. Manuscript of a commentary on Ibn Sīnā's *Pointers and Reminders* by Najm al-Dīn al-Nakhjuwānī.

request from friends for a brief exposition of philosophy. It is mostly cobbled together from his own earlier writings, including a likewise synoptic work, the *Philosophy for 'Arūḍī* (*al-Ḥikma al-'Arūḍiyya*). In the later Islamic tradition, the most widely discussed text of this kind was the *Pointers and Reminders* (*al-Ishārāt wa-l-tanbīhāt*) (Figure 2). As with *The Fair Judgement*, the title is a good guide to Ibn Sīnā's approach, as the *Pointers* is written in a highly allusive and compressed fashion. It seems that the purpose of this was to exercise the reader, who should know Ibn Sīnā's doctrines from reading his other treatises or studying with him personally, and use the hints provided to reconstruct full syllogisms in confirmation of these doctrines. The latter context also produced the *Notes* (*al-Ta'līqāt*) and *Discussions* (*al-Mubāḥathāt*), the latter of which transmits questions and answers between Ibn Sīnā and his two students Ibn Zayla and Bahmanyār.

In addition, we have a number of treatises on specific philosophical themes, like the soul (the subject of his earliest extant work), ethics, the afterlife, and love (*ʿishq*). His treatise on the latter topic shows the importance of Neoplatonism for Ibn Sīnā, even if his writings usually do not wear their Plotinian inspiration on their sleeves, in comparison to an author like Miskawayh. It understands love as a cosmic phenomenon in which all things pursue individual goods in an attempt to revert back upon their perfect source, God. Finally, Ibn Sīnā's constant experimentation as an author also led him to write allegorical narratives like *Ḥayy Ibn Yaqẓān*, whose title was borrowed by the 12th-century Andalusian author Ibn Ṭufayl for a more famous treatise of the same name. In Ibn Sīnā's work the title character (whose name literally means 'Living, son of awake') is a philosopher who visits the different parts of the cosmos, representing the soul's journey to God. Scholarship is still needed on the relation between these parables, his treatises on individual themes, and the longer synoptic treatises that have attracted the lion's share of attention from readers from Ibn Sīnā's death to the present day.

Commentaries on the *Pointers*

In the Latin scholastic tradition, *The Healing* was Ibn Sīnā's most widely consulted philosophical work, which makes sense given its thoroughness and clear relation to Aristotelianism, which was of central interest to the scholastics. In the Islamic world, by contrast, the most popular work was the dense and challenging *Pointers and Reminders*. These very features made it a perfect text for commentary. Being so hard to understand, it positively called out for exegesis, and its relative brevity meant it could be quoted fully before the commentator went on to expound his own thoughts at length. Two sharply contrasting commentaries were written in the late 12th and 13th centuries, by Fakhr al-Dīn al-Rāzī

(d. 1210) and Naṣīr al-Dīn al-Ṭūsī (d. 1274). Fakhr al-Dīn was highly critical, posing every objection he could think of—and he was very good at thinking of objections. Even where he agreed with Ibn Sīnā's conclusions, he tried to offer improved arguments for those conclusions. Al-Ṭūsī's commentary is largely a response which rises to Ibn Sīnā's defence, and thus a kind of 'super-commentary'.

These were only two of many responses to the *Pointers*. A study of philosophical commentary up to the year 1900 counts about 20 commentaries on it, several of which received super-commentaries. It was thus the first instance of a key development in the post-classical Islamic world. Philosophers frequently expressed their ideas by writing glosses or line-by-line commentaries on a standard 'base-text' (*matn*). To some extent post-classical philosophy in the Islamic world can be divided in terms of the dominance of a given base-text in a given time period or place. Later examples of major base-texts, which often shared the brevity and compression of the *Pointers*, would be al-Ṭūsī's own *Tajrīd al-ʿaqāʾid* (*Disclosure of Doctrines*: it even generated fourth-level commentaries), somewhat later, al-Ījī's *Mawāqif fī ʿilm al-kalām* (*Stations of Theology*), and in the modern era the *Sullam al-ʿulūm* (*Ladder of the Sciences*) of al-Bihārī, a work that received many commentaries in Muslim India.

Chapter 2
Logic and knowledge

In his diatribes against hated rival Abū l-Qāsim al-Kirmānī, Ibn Sīnā stooped to verbal abuse. But he had more principled objections to al-Kirmānī's way of doing philosophy, which he expressed in a letter to other members of the Baghdad school: this man did not know how to mount arguments, but offered merely dialectical proofs. Ibn Sīnā was not going to make the same mistake. As we saw, he spent his youth mapping out his burgeoning knowledge in the form of syllogistic arguments, in an attempt to capture science in the form of adamantine chains of demonstration. Like Aristotle before him, Ibn Sīnā did not fill his works with relentless lists of syllogisms. His authorial methods were instead adapted to the pedagogical needs of his readership. Yet his entire philosophy presupposes a theory of scientific demonstration, which undergirds his epistemology in general and in particular such famous arguments as his flying man thought experiment and his proof for the existence of God.

Terms, propositions, and demonstrations

As in other areas, Ibn Sīnā's work on logic was broadly within an Aristotelian framework, but made numerous fundamental innovations within that framework. This was true even when it came to the topics to be covered within logic. Since late antiquity, Aristotle's logical writings had been collected as the so-called

Organon (meaning 'instrument'), which included much more than what we'd call logic nowadays. It spans from Aristotle's *Categories*, which offers an exhaustive list of the types of single term (substance terms like 'human' and 'horse', qualitative terms like 'black' and 'cold', etc.), to the *Poetics* and *Rhetoric*. For Ibn Sīnā the core of the *Organon* was to be found in the *Prior* and *Posterior Analytics*, which respectively study valid syllogistic arguments and the special case of syllogisms called 'demonstrations'. Only demonstrative proofs are suitable for use in science. (In fact the Arabic title of the *Posterior Analytics* was just *al-Burhān*, meaning *Demonstration*; this is also the title of the corresponding part of Ibn Sīnā's *The Healing*.) Ibn Sīnā went so far as to dismiss the value of the categories for logic. He grudgingly included a section on it in *The Healing* but warned that this was only out of deference to standard practice.

For Ibn Sīnā we get into logic proper only once we are dealing with objects of two mental operations called 'conception' (*taṣawwur*) and 'assent' (*taṣdīq*). This distinction, with the same terminology, was already used by al-Fārābī. To have a 'conception' of a term is just to grasp what the term means, a grasp that could be expressed in a definition. All competent language users have *some* conception of any given term. If the term in question is 'giraffe', they will reliably be able to distinguish giraffes from non-giraffes, and will be able to explain roughly what they mean by the word 'giraffe'. They might say, 'a giraffe is that tall animal that lopes around on the savannah'. But this will only be a nominal definition, a mere 'description' (*rasm*). A real definition (*ḥadd*) is one that captures what it really means to fall under the relevant term, for instance, what exactly makes something a giraffe. These are the sorts of definition suitable for use in science.

Some conceptions build on others: presumably we need to have a conception of 'animal' before we can arrive at a conception of 'giraffe'. But on pain of infinite regress, there must be some conceptions that are primitive or primary. These will not be grasped, or explained, by appealing to any other term. Notable examples appear in Ibn Sīnā's metaphysics, where he says that 'thing' and 'existent' are such primary notions. Likewise the modal properties of necessity, contingency, and impossibility. You can explain them in terms of each other if you want, as by saying that the contingent (*mumkin*) is that which is neither necessary nor impossible. Or you could paraphrase, in a rather circular fashion: the contingent is what might be, but needn't be. But precisely because this would be circular, it is not a definition or explanation. It is just a way of calling attention to the listener's tacit understanding of what contingency is.

One can have a conception without asserting anything, not even that anything exists that corresponds to the conception. Ibn Sīnā mentions the case of empty space or 'void': he argues that there is no void, but he still has a conception of it. Indeed, how could one go about arguing against the existence of void without having a conception of it? But in logic we are mostly interested in conceptions because they can be combined to form assertions or 'assents', which can be either positive ('giraffe is ungulate') or negative ('giraffe is not stone'). Just as there are immediate conceptions, so there are cases of immediate assent, propositions to which we agree as soon as we understand their meaning, and which are not justified by anything further. This is for the same reason as in the case of conceptions: to avoid an endless regress where all propositions depend on further propositions. Anyone should assent to an immediate proposition as soon as attention is called to it. Ibn Sīnā calls this a 'reminder' (*tanbīh*), a word we already saw in the title of his *Pointers and Reminders*.

Which is not to say that there is no room for confusion. Some beliefs are so generally accepted that they may *seem* to be self-evident, whereas in fact they are not. To test whether something is a genuine first principle, Ibn Sīnā suggests considering whether someone will assent to it regardless of their personal history. For instance, 'justice is admirable' may look like a first principle of moral reasoning, but Ibn Sīnā denies this, on the grounds that someone from a corrupt society may find it doubtful. By contrast, something like 'the whole is greater than the part' is obviously true, and will command the assent of any competent rational being. This is a pretty strict standard, and doesn't give us much to work with as a stock of certainly true propositions. But Ibn Sīnā does recognize other ways of arriving at certain assent without needing an argument. You might just grasp something with the senses, for instance. He also accepts that the accumulation of reliable testimony (*tawātur*) may be a source of certain knowledge. This looks like a concession to the Islamic religious sciences, which invoked testimony as the means by which, for instance, later generations know things about the Prophet Muḥammad, despite never having met him in person.

We also find ourselves believing things even when we don't know them for sure. An important category of such beliefs is the 'widely accepted' (*mashhūr*). These are propositions people normally agree with, even without proof, and even without being certain of their truth. In some circumstances it is perfectly fine to argue from such premises, for instance if you are just trying to win an argument. This is what one does when practising dialectic, an art explored by both Aristotle and Ibn Sīnā in great detail. What one should avoid, though, is confusing dialectical argument with genuine demonstration. That was the mistake committed by al-Kirmānī, and Ibn Sīnā thought that theologians were typically guilty of the same blunder.

A demonstration will take the form of a syllogism which, as Ibn Sīnā puts it, echoing Aristotle's definition, is 'an argument in which, if more than one thing is posited, something other than what was posited follows from these things by necessity, and not accidentally, but essentially'. In other words, we will have more than one premise, and the premises together will imply a conclusion. Notice that this definition does not require that the premises and conclusion are *true*, only that the conclusion does validly follow. But the process is truth-preserving, meaning that true premises will yield a true conclusion. Likewise, if we *know* the premises to be true, we can use the syllogism to generate new knowledge, namely of the conclusion. In practice this will take one of two forms. First, the kinds of syllogisms considered by Aristotle, where terms are predicated of subjects, as in the following:

Hoofed is said of ungulate
Ungulate is said of giraffe
Therefore hoofed is said of giraffe.

Second, the hypothetical arguments not considered by Aristotle, but dealt with by the Stoics and integrated into Aristotelian logic already by late ancient commentators. For instance:

If it is night-time, the giraffe is sleeping
It is night-time
Therefore the giraffe is sleeping.

Ibn Sīnā explicitly argues that hypotheticals still satisfy Aristotle's general definition of the syllogism, and considers them in his logical writings. But following the *Posterior Analytics*, he thinks that demonstrative science is concerned above all with syllogisms whose premises and conclusions are predications.

One reason for this is that such syllogisms have 'middle terms', like 'ungulate' in the above example. The middle binds together the extreme terms (here 'hoofed' and 'giraffe') and explains the predication in the conclusion: it is *because* giraffes are ungulates that they are hoofed. Ibn Sīnā thus thinks that science involves the search for explanatory middle terms. ('I wonder why giraffes have hooves?') The moment of insight at which the middle term is discovered ('oh, I see, it is because they are ungulates!') is called 'intuition' (*ḥads*). Someone gifted with effortless and plentiful intuitions is said to have 'acumen' (*dhakāʾ*). This frees them from the burden of laboriously 'thinking' (*fikr*) about what might explain the phenomenon in question. In the extreme case, someone who is 'incandescent with intuition' possesses a power Ibn Sīnā calls the 'sacred faculty'. He associates this with prophethood.

While this goes considerably beyond Aristotle's *Posterior Analytics*, it is recognizably based on that work, as is Ibn Sīnā's demand that demonstrations be necessary in character and universal in scope. The biologist who specializes in giraffes is not out to understand why this giraffe standing in front of her happens to be hoofed, but why *all* giraffes are hoofed, and *must* be hoofed. Even if we can have certainty about something particular and contingent, as when we know through testimony that Muḥammad existed and said certain things, this sort of knowledge will not feature in the demonstrative syllogisms that make up science. Ibn Sīnā is also far clearer than earlier logicians on the difference between something's *always* being the case and its *necessarily* being the case. Suppose it just so happens that no giraffe ever visits Antarctica. This would not make it impossible that a giraffe visit Antarctica. For the same reason, it is not the same to say that something is possible and to say that it happens at least once.

Having distinguished these kinds of 'modality' (never/sometimes/always and impossible/possible/necessary) Ibn Sīnā is able to extend Aristotle's logic by considering what happens when we combine statements with the different modalities. For instance, if you combine a 'necessity' premise with an 'always' premise, will the conclusion hold necessarily, or merely always? He also observes that all predicative statements must have one or another modality, even if it is not expressed. Thus when I say 'all giraffes are ungulates' this really means '*necessarily*, all giraffes are ungulates', whereas when I say 'all giraffes sleep' this might mean 'all giraffes are *sometimes* asleep' or 'all giraffes are *possibly* asleep'.

Prophecy

One of the bolder moves made by the *falāsifa* was to 'naturalize' the central phenomenon of Islamic religion: prophecy. Since they held that the perfect philosopher is one who has complete knowledge of all 'intelligibles', they assumed that the prophet must be someone who gets this same knowledge but in a less laborious fashion. Ibn Sīnā pushes this standard *falsafa* view to its limits by integrating prophecy directly into his theory of syllogistic discovery. He recognizes several kinds of prophecy, the greatest of which is nothing other than the 'sacred faculty', which allows for the quick and prolific finding of middle terms. On this basis Ibn Sīnā even develops a novel argument for the necessity of prophecy. Given that some people have no intuition at all, and are so minimally gifted in this respect, it only stands to reason that other people will be maximally capable of intuition. These are the people who have the sacred faculty.

In addition to this psychological argument for the sacred faculty, which is found in the treatise on soul in *The Healing*, Ibn Sīnā offers a political argument for why there must be prophecy more generally. This comes near the end of the treatise on metaphysics in the same work. Since humans are communal animals, who live in societies kept in order by laws, they need a lawgiver. This will be someone who understands what will be good for the community and can institute rules that ensure these goods will be achieved. Since humans stand in need of such individuals, divine providence will provide them. Ibn Sīnā here emphasizes the limited doctrinal content of the prophet's message. It is aimed at securing justice and harmony between people, not disseminating knowledge about God or anything else. In this respect prophecy should restrict itself to teaching monotheism and the afterlife. To insist on more would just sow confusion amongst common believers. This seems a clear dig at the theologians, who did discuss such fine points, claiming to base themselves on the revelation. On the other hand, the prophetic message may also use 'symbols' to call select people towards philosophical investigation (*al-baḥth al-ḥikmī*). With this, Ibn Sīnā quietly anticipates Ibn Rushd's later claim, made in his famous *Decisive Treatise*, that Islam exhorts and even requires those with sufficient talent to pursue philosophy.

Another important feature of Ibn Sīnā's logic makes it more flexible than Aristotle's. He distinguishes between what later came to be called 'substantial' (*dhātī*) and 'descriptional' (*waṣfī*) interpretations of a proposition. A predicate holds of its subject 'substantially' if it is true of it whenever it exists, whereas a predicate holds 'descriptionally' if it is true only under some condition. For example 'all moving things are changing position' looks straightforwardly true at first glance. But in fact it does not hold substantially, only descriptionally. A given moving thing, like a giraffe, is changing position *so long as it moves*, but not whenever the giraffe exists.

This looks like a small, even pedantic point. But it is in fact of tremendous importance, since it allows Ibn Sīnā to expand greatly the scope of premises that can satisfy the strictures of Aristotelian demonstration. Once we allow propositions that are true only descriptionally, we can admit into science propositions that are true only on some condition or assumption. It is always and necessarily true, for example, that things are changing position *assuming that* they are moving. This breaks the link that had long been made in Aristotelian philosophy between necessity and eternity. What is necessarily true of giraffes *might* tell us about permanent features of the world, if it is true of giraffes substantially, and if there are always giraffes. A proposition like 'giraffes are ungulates' would satisfy these criteria.

But it is also necessarily true of giraffes that they are changing position when moving, and this does not require that giraffes are always (or even frequently) moving. It would, on Ibn Sīnā's view, be enough for one giraffe to move just once.

Now, as we'll be seeing in Chapter 5, Ibn Sīnā was an eternalist. That is, he believed that the universe has always existed and always will. But he did not say this in order to guarantee that science can discover permanently necessary truths. Given the availability of merely descriptive yet necessary propositions, there could be such truths even if the universe existed only for a limited time. Rather, the universe is eternal because it is always caused to exist *extrinsically*, by God. In itself, neither the universe nor anything in it has any claim to eternity. Thus our scientific conclusions about things other than God never presuppose that they *must* exist. Even so, those conclusions are necessary truths, founded upon other necessary truths, via chains of inferences that derive ultimately from immediate first principles.

Essentialism and science

The reason for Ibn Sīnā's interest in necessity in demonstration is that, again following Aristotle, he thinks proper science should be an investigation of the essential properties of things. (There are several Arabic terms for 'essence', including *dhāt*, *māhiyya*, and *ḥaqīqa*.) A property holds essentially of a subject if the subject by its very nature cannot lack that property. In such cases it is the subject's nature that underwrites the necessity of the predication. This can happen with both substantial and merely descriptive truths: giraffes are essentially ungulates, and moving things are *as such* (that is, *as moving things*) essentially by changing position. All other properties are mere accidents (*aʿrāḍ*). For instance, 'giraffes are in Africa' is accidentally true, since it doesn't need to be true whenever giraffes exist; and 'moving thing is a giraffe' is accidentally true, since a moving thing *as such* does not need to be a giraffe.

But for Ibn Sīnā, not all essential properties are created equal. He made yet another fundamental distinction between 'constituent' (*muqawwim*) and 'concomitant' (*lāzim*) essential properties. Constituents are included in the very conceptualization of a term. In other words, if X is a constituent of S, we cannot even conceive of an S that is not X. In the first instance this means the notions that appear in a real definition, like 'animal' and 'ungulate' for giraffe. (To my shame I'm not sure what the definition of 'giraffe' is, but I suppose it would include these two terms.) The constituents would furthermore include terms that are higher up in the logical tree, to use a metaphor that goes nicely with our chosen example. For instance, if ungulates are a sub-species of mammals, then by mentioning 'ungulate' in the definition we have implicitly included 'mammal' as a constituent, and likewise 'animal', since 'mammal' falls under this still more general term. Nonetheless it's obvious that the constituents will be relatively few in number and not very informative. These are the features of giraffes that we get 'for free' just by knowing what giraffes are.

So most of the action in science has to do with the essential or necessary concomitants (*lawāzim*, also *lawāḥiq*). As the name says, these are features that *follow* from the essence but do not *constitute* it. To use examples given by Ibn Sīnā, being able to laugh is a concomitant of human being, since this follows from being rational; burning is a concomitant of fire, since this follows from being hot; and it is a concomitant of triangle that its internal angles add up to 180 degrees, since this can be proven on the basis of its definition. Noticing the invariant features of things and tracing these features back to the definitions that express essences is the main task of scientific inquiry. The relation may be rather indirect, if we have to go through numerous middle terms back to the essence. For instance, a more remote concomitant of triangle is having half the internal degrees of a square (180 is half of 360), which follows from the more proximate concomitant just mentioned. But as long as we can construct chains of syllogisms that ultimately ground a property in the essence, the property is a necessary concomitant.

Ibn Sīnā believes that one may 'conceive' of a subject as lacking its necessary concomitant, unlike a constituent; but one cannot 'imagine' it as lacking the concomitant. The point being, again, that the constituents make up our very understanding of giraffe, triangle, fire, etc., whereas the essential concomitants are not like this, but are still invariant features these things must always have. All other properties are merely accidental. Now, it might just happen that a mere accident is possessed in all cases. Suppose that no giraffes ever wind up existing outside Africa. Then 'being in Africa' would always be predicated of giraffes, but it would still not be essential or necessary of giraffes that they cannot exist outside Africa. (Confusingly, Ibn Sīnā uses the word 'concomitant' for this case also, which is why I have been speaking of *essential* or *necessary* concomitants.) This is why one could easily imagine a giraffe in Japan, even if in fact no giraffes ever existed outside Africa.

The upshot is that our approach to the properties of things needs to be sensitive to the type of property at stake. If it is a constituent, we need only consult our conception to see whether it belongs. Perhaps someone can help us to do this by offering a 'pointer' or 'reminder', but it cannot be demonstrated. This makes sense: if you don't understand that giraffe is animal or ungulate, no one can prove it to you, because you don't even know what a giraffe is. By contrast, if the property in question is an essential concomitant, we should try to tie it back to the essence through demonstrative syllogisms, explaining *why* it belongs thanks to the middle terms. If it is a mere accident, this will not be possible, even if by chance the accident happens to belong in every case. Again, this makes sense: how could you prove demonstratively that no giraffes are ever in Antarctica, given that this does not follow from their essential nature and so could have been otherwise?

Everything just explained would apply to any science, not only the study of giraffes. Actually, I regret to say that the study of giraffes is not even the most important of sciences. That position is reserved for metaphysics, which is the highest of sciences, in the sense that all other scientific disciplines are subordinated to it. One science is subordinated to another if the former takes principles from the latter. For example, astronomy is subordinated to geometry, since the astronomer simply assumes many things proven by the geometer. Whereas metaphysics, the highest science, is maximally general—it studies all existents insofar as they exist—lower sciences are narrower in focus. Thus astronomy studies not all geometrical shapes but only spheres, because it examines the features of heavenly bodies, which for Ibn Sīnā are rotating spheres (more on this later). Furthermore, astronomy studies spheres specifically insofar as they are in circular motion; otherwise it would just be the part of geometry that deals with spheres.

Notice the connection here to the above point about propositions that are true 'descriptionally': the truths of astronomy will apply to spheres *provided that* they are moving. In particular, the astronomer will demonstrate the necessary concomitant features of spheres in circular motion, such as that they must always return to their original position after one rotation. This applies no less to the case of metaphysics, where the task is to investigate the concomitants of the existence as such, for instance cause and effect, actuality and potentiality, necessity and possibility, and universality and particularity.

Sensation and intellection

This very contrast between universality and particularity is fundamental to another part of Ibn Sīnā's epistemology, where he explains the different kinds of cognition we can perform. As we've seen, demonstration concerns itself with universal, necessary truths about a given subject matter, the subject matter relevant to whichever scientific discipline is at hand. At the logical level, this means having a conceptualization of each subject matter that can be expressed as a real definition, and then on that basis demonstrating how further properties (the concomitants) belong to the subject matter. At the psychological level, it means engaging in intellection (*'aql*), which is a function of the rational faculty or power of the soul. We then have other powers that allow us to deal with particulars, the most obvious being sensation (*ḥiss*). For instance, I grasp universal truths about giraffes using intellection, but use eyesight to grasp that this particular giraffe is running.

We'll learn more about these powers and their interrelation in the next chapter. For now let's focus on what contribution sensation makes to human knowledge. The first thing to note is that we can know things directly via the senses. Remember, sensation is one source of certain assent: under normal conditions, when I see the particular giraffe running I can take myself to be sure that she is running. Unfortunately, this is not going to be enough to get me to truths suitable for use in science. How do I make the leap from seeing and hearing particulars to knowing things at a universal level, something Ibn Sīnā would describe as moving from a grasp of the 'sensible' (*maḥsūs*) to a grasp of the 'intelligible' (*ma'qūl*)? Here we run into a problem, which is not that Ibn Sīnā fails to give an answer to our question, but that he seems to give *two* answers.

The first answer, which is broadly speaking familiar from late ancient discussions of Aristotle, is to invoke 'abstraction' (*tajrīd*). The idea here would be to take our sensible image gleaned from particular giraffes and to purify it, by eliminating anything not essential to giraffes. Forget that it is in Japan, or eating hay. These are mere accidents. Focus just on the fact that it is an animal, an ungulate, etc. We should be left with a conception that applies universally to all giraffes, which as we know is the needed foundation for scientific inquiry.

The second answer instead invokes 'emanation' (*fayḍ*), and here somewhat more explanation will be needed. As we'll see when we come to talking about those heavenly bodies, Ibn Sīnā believed that there are celestial intellects associated with the spheres, which descend from God in a necessary chain of emanations, like lights giving rise to further lights or like a fountain with water overflowing from one level to the next. This represents a fusion of classical Neoplatonism, which is where the 'emanation' metaphor comes from, with Aristotelian cosmology. Ibn Sīnā takes the whole picture from al-Fārābī, who also proposed that the lowest of the celestial spheres, the so-called Active Intellect, is somehow involved in activating the potential for knowledge in human knowers, just as it is involved in bestowing form on suitably prepared matter. Ibn Sīnā takes over this idea, agreeing with al-Fārābī that intelligibles are emanated into the human mind. So this too could explain how we have knowledge of sufficient generality and necessity to do science.

How then should we deal with the fact that Ibn Sīnā seems to have accounted for this twice, first 'from below' through an abstractive process based on sensation, then 'from above' through emanation from the Active Intellect? That turns out to be one of the most controversial questions in modern scholarship on Ibn Sīnā. It seems obvious at least that sensation provides a prompt for acquiring knowledge. If humans never empirically encountered giraffes, of course they could not do science about them. But for emanation to play a role, it seems that sensation cannot be enough. One idea might be that sensory input lacks the universality and necessity required by Ibn Sīnā's theory of demonstration, and that the emanated intelligible somehow provides this. If this or something like it is right, then sensation is only a trigger which brings on the really key event, which is the arrival of the intelligible. Abstraction *prepares* you to know something in a universal way, but emanation actually makes you do it. In favour of this idea is that it would be pleasingly similar to the way matter receives form from the Active Intellect when the matter is ready. And there is some good textual evidence for it, as when Ibn Sīnā says, 'perception conveys to the soul things that are

The Active Intellect

Against stiff competition, the most baffling and most-discussed passage in Aristotle is probably book three, chapter five of his treatise *On the Soul*. Having just discussed the human capacity for intellection, Aristotle goes on to say that there must be a productive active intellect to complement the potential intellect just described. Whereas the potential intellect 'becomes' things by thinking about them, this intellect 'makes' things, and is like a light, apparently because it somehow enables the potential intellect to become actual. Commentators in late antiquity and the Islamic world wrestled with this chapter, variously concluding that it describes an aspect of the human soul, a superhuman mind, or even God. The *falāsifa* mostly took the second option: Aristotle was describing an intellect superior to the individual human mind, but inferior to God. This already seems to be the idea of al-Kindī in his brief treatise *On the Intellect*. But it was al-Fārābī who prepared the way for Ibn Sīnā's understanding of the issue. For al-Fārābī, the 'Active Intellect' is identified with the celestial intellect connected to the lowest celestial sphere, the one on which the Moon is seated.

With respect to our lower world below the Moon, the Active Intellect has two analogous functions. First, it is the 'giver of forms' (*wāhib al-ṣuwar*), forms that are received wherever matter is suitably prepared, like a radio signal that becomes audible wherever a device is tuned correctly. Thus when, for instance, matter is prepared in the womb of a female animal, the relevant species form will be received from the Active Intellect, yielding the offspring. Which makes it far easier to explain the supposed phenomenon of spontaneous generation. No parent is needed, since flies, worms, and the like can be brought out of rotting matter when the matter happens to develop aptitude for receiving an emanated form. Ibn Sīnā thought that in principle, this could occur with higher animals, even humans. It's just that the suitable preparation of matter is far less likely to occur. Second, and as implied by Aristotle, the Active Intellect is involved in actualizing the human potential for knowledge. This helps to undergird Ibn Sīnā's epistemological optimism. The things in the world around us were given their natures by the same source that is somehow allowing us to know those natures, which guarantees a correspondence between things in the mind and things in the world.

mixed and unintelligible, and the intellect makes them intelligible'. But other interpretations have been defended. For example, emanation might be needed to explain how we can know about things when particulars are not available, as the giraffe scientist can do demonstrations about giraffes even if she is not looking at one. If this is right, then we get knowledge initially through abstraction, but are able to return to what we know through emanation.

In any case, one way or another sensation does seem to be required for successful intellection. So we might wonder whether it would be fair to describe Ibn Sīnā as an empiricist. The answer is no, at least if we take 'empiricism' to mean the view that all knowledge is acquired from sensation. That would be especially evident on views which give a greater role to emanation in his epistemology. But even leaving that aside, Ibn Sīnā makes it clear that the intellect grasps many things on its own, without getting them from the senses. Immediate conceptions fall into this category. He says that such notions as 'existent', 'thing', 'cause', and so on, as well as laws of reasoning like the principle of non-contradiction, 'transcend the realm of perception'. The same would go for cases of immediate assent like 'the whole is greater than the part', about which Ibn Sīnā explicitly says that even if the conceptions 'whole', 'greater', and 'part' are taken from sensation, the assent to the principle itself does *not* come from sensation but from our inborn disposition to make the judgement (*jibilla*).

One might retrench here to the claim that Ibn Sīnā is an empiricist in a weaker sense. He may believe that sensation is not a source, but a *necessary precondition* for knowledge, even if the intellect is active on its own at the prompting of sense experience, as when it assents to first principles. While that would not make him an 'empiricist' in the stronger sense of this term usually employed in the history of philosophy and applied to figures like Locke, Berkeley, and Hume, it would mean that he agrees with them that a mind that has never enjoyed sense-experience would simply be 'blank', or in Aristotelian terms wholly potential. In Ibn Sīnā's terms, it would have no conceptions or assents. But as it turns out, no pre-modern philosopher denies this more explicitly than Ibn Sīnā. In his famous flying man thought experiment, to be discussed in Chapter 3, he takes it to be not just true but *obvious* that a person who has never had any sensory input at all will assent to something, namely the proposition that they exist. From this I conclude that Ibn Sīnā was not an empiricist, in either a strong or weak sense. But it remains true that *almost* all knowledge for Ibn Sīnā is at least prompted by sensation, if not drawn from sensation. So in practice, his scientific method is for the most part indistinguishable from what an empiricist might recommend.

Chapter 3
The human person

We have already dipped our toes into the deep waters of Ibn Sīnā's philosophical anthropology. Central to his epistemology was the contrast between cognition aimed at intelligibles, performed by the rational soul, and cognition aimed at particulars, performed by the senses. We're now going to find out that he recognized other powers, seated in the brain, that deal with particulars and thus fall short of full-blown intellection, but are less tied to the immediate physical environment than sensation. These further powers belong to animals, as well as humans. The rational soul remains doubly set apart, as unique to humans and separate from matter. Indeed, for Ibn Sīnā it is our possession of reason or intellect that proves we can survive bodily death.

Faculty psychology

From classical antiquity, philosophers of the Islamic world inherited two theories concerning the complexity of the human soul. From Plato they had the idea that each person has three 'parts' to their soul or even three 'souls', namely reason, spirit, and desire. The modern reader will probably associate this especially with Plato's *Republic* but the account best known in Arabic was the one in his *Timaeus*. The leading medical authority Galen was a conduit for this account, so it was well known to figures who worked in medicine, like Ibn Sīnā. The second theory

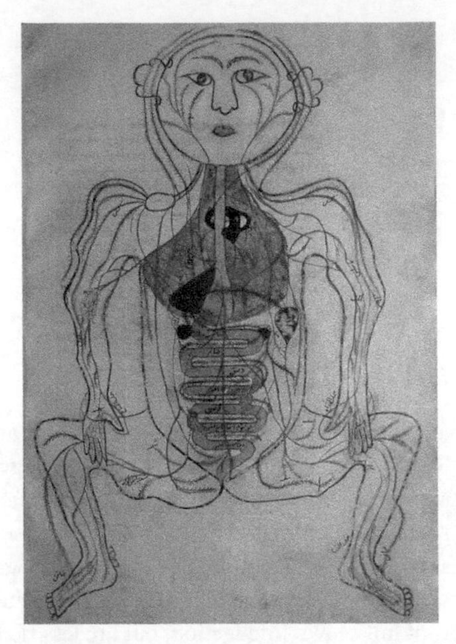

3. Illustration of the venous system from a manuscript of Ibn Ilyās' *Anatomy of the Human Body*.

was that of Aristotle, who recognized three sets of psychological faculties:

> *Nutrition, growth, reproduction*: belong to plants, animals, and humans
>
> *Sensation, voluntary motion*: belong to animals and humans
>
> *Rational thought*: belongs only to humans

In Arabic philosophical works the two theories were often conflated: plants have only a 'desiring' soul (since they partake in reproduction and nutrition, which are typical of this soul), non-human animals have the 'spirit' (since they are capable of emotions but not thinking), and of course humans are distinguished by reason.

While this satisfied the urge to find harmony between the two great authorities, the conflation is not really that convincing. This is clear if we consider the souls of animals. True, animals can get angry, a function of the Platonic 'spirit'. But for Aristotle what is really distinctive about animals is not emotion. It is the psychological powers or faculties (Greek *dunameis*, Arabic *quwan*) that differentiate them from plants. Aristotle's 'faculty psychology', his focus on the abilities or capacities distinctive of each kind of soul, goes well with his famous definition of soul as 'the perfection of the body that potentially has life'. Each species of plant and animal, and the human species, is marked out by a specific kind of form, and the form confers certain capacities and dispositions on the living thing. Ibn Sīnā's own psychological theory strikes a balance here. On the one hand he develops his own faculty psychology, which builds on Aristotle's. On the other hand he criticizes Aristotle's definition of soul and adopts a robust dualism, according to which the human soul is in itself immaterial and thus capable of existing without the body.

Aristotle was well aware that human and animal mental life involves more than just sensation and intellection. We dream, remember, recollect, imagine, and so on. He discussed these functions, but without carefully distinguishing different faculties responsible for them. It would be a little unfair, but only a little, to say that he simply bracketed them under the catch-all heading of *phantasia*, which is sometimes translated as 'imagination' but in fact ranges across the aforementioned phenomena. By the time we get to Ibn Sīnā things look very different. He draws upon subsequent authors, especially Galen, to develop an account of what he calls the 'internal senses'. There are five of them, to match the number of external senses:

Challenges for the faculty psychology

It might seem that the biggest threat to Ibn Sīnā's faculty psychology would be the apparently rather arbitrary division between the faculties. Just as he divided up the functions of Aristotle's *phantasia* among multiple 'internal senses', so someone might wonder whether Ibn Sīnā's faculties could be further subdivided. Maybe there is one power of touch for temperature and another for pleasure and pain, or a distinct visual power for seeing each colour? Anticipating this objection, Ibn Sīnā insists that his enumeration of faculties is correct, and that each faculty is distinguished from the others by its 'primary purpose', like the seeing of colour. Individual applications of the faculty are derivations or 'branches' (*furūʿ*) from that central activity.

What he does not seem to have anticipated is that later authors would attack from the other direction. Especially two 12th-century thinkers, Abū l-Barakāt al-Baghdādī and Fakhr al-Dīn al-Rāzī, questioned the whole project of faculty psychology. They urged that the subject of cognition is not a sense organ or a ventricle of the brain, nor is it a power seated in these parts of the body. Instead, the subject of *all* my cognitions, from sensation all the way up to intellection, is just me. Fakhr al-Dīn gives a powerful argument against Ibn Sīnā's theory. Just as I can judge that honey is both yellow and sweet, a function of the common sense, so I can see Zayd with my eyes while understanding that he falls under the universal intelligible *human*. If we need to posit a unified power, the common sense, to handle the honey case, then we need to posit a unified subject of both my eyesight and my intellectual deployment of universal concepts. Otherwise I would not be able to make the single judgement 'Zayd who I am seeing falls under the universal *human*.' This argument threatens to undo the complexity of Ibn Sīnā's psychology. Yet it may ironically enough be inspired by his own reflections on self-awareness, discussed later in this chapter. Ibn Sīnā's critics took his idea of a single subject that is *aware* of all cognition and modified it, positing a single subject that *performs* all cognition.

(a) *Common sense* (*al-ḥiss al-mushtarak*). It combines what is given by the external senses, as when different properties are perceived as belonging to the same thing (Aristotle already gave the example of grasping that honey is both sweet and yellow), or putting together impressions received at consecutive times, as when we see a falling raindrop as a line.

(b) *Imaginative store* (*al-khayāl* or *al-muṣawwira*). It preserves images received by the external senses and common sense, and those produced by the imagination.

(c) *Wahm*. It grasps properties of particular items in the environment that are not available to sense-perception.

(d) *Memorative store* (*al-dhikr* or *al-ḥāfiẓa*). It preserves features of things that have been grasped by the *wahm*.

(e) *Imagination* (*al-mutakhayyila*). It manipulates images gleaned from sense perception and the *wahm*, by 'separating and combining' them (think of conjuring up the image of a centaur or Pegasus).

Just as the external senses are seated in bodily organs, for instance sight in the eyes, so these 'senses' are seated in the body, namely in five different parts of the brain. This supposedly explains why people with different head injuries are variously affected in their cognition. Also like the external senses, the internal senses only ever deal with particulars. Even when you imagine something unreal, like a centaur, you are combining *particular* sense impressions (a human, a horse) to get a *particular* imaginative image. Universal thinking is reserved for the rational soul, which is not seated in any bodily organ.

Apart from its systematicity, the most novel aspect of this theory is the third power on the list, *wahm*. It is usually translated into English as 'estimation', following the lead of medieval Latin translators who rendered it as *aestimatio*. But this is rather misleading, since that English word suggests guessing or approximation. In fact what *wahm* does is to grasp certain properties of things which belong to perceptible things but are not themselves perceptible, at least not by the external senses. These properties are, somewhat unhelpfully, called *maʿānī* in Arabic—the plural of *maʿnā*, a famously untranslatable word that can convey the notion of 'meaning', 'object', 'feature', and so on. The best way to explain what they are is to give an example. Ibn Sīnā does just that, offering an illustration that becomes ubiquitous in later philosophy in both Arabic and Latin (it even turns up in Descartes). Suppose a sheep encounters a wolf. The sheep can use its eyes to see the colour of the wolf's coat, and its nose to smell the wolf. But what it most urgently needs to do is perceive that the wolf is dangerous or, as Ibn Sīnā puts it, 'hostile'. Which is exactly what the sheep does, leading it to run for safety. Conversely animals use *wahm* to perceive the familiarity or friendliness of conspecifics, like their own offspring. *Wahm*, then, is responsible for perceiving properties of sensible things inaccessible to eyesight, hearing, etc.

Ibn Sīnā's postulation of this faculty shows his concern to account for the behaviour of non-human animals, befitting a man who included a lengthy treatise on zoology in *The Healing*. It is remarkable how much overlap he sees between humans and animals, or at least the higher animals that have fully developed external and internal senses. As al-Ghazālī would later observe, one might take from Ibn Sīnā the idea that humans are just animals with a rational soul added on top. This isn't strictly accurate, since we can use reason to deploy the imagination in ways animals can't. When we do this the power is called 'cogitative' (*mufakkira*), which is what we use, for instance, to plan what to have for dinner. Cogitation involves manipulating representations of particulars ('maybe that leftover tofu in the fridge?') and so is clearly not a function of the intellect. Nonetheless, by granting so much cognitive sophistication to animals, Ibn Sīnā has partly closed the gap Aristotle and other philosophers posited as separating humans and non-humans.

The incorporeality of the rational soul

But only partly. Among earthly beings, humans are special because they alone have immaterial souls that can survive the death of their bodies. Ibn Sīnā is therefore unsatisfied with the aforementioned Aristotelian definition that makes the soul a form or 'perfection' of the body. In the opening chapter of his treatise on the soul in *The Healing*, Ibn Sīnā allows that this is not entirely wrong. Your soul is a 'perfection' of the body in the sense that it is the source of the body's perfections and activities. It would even be fair to say that the word 'soul' (*nafs*) applies specifically to this entity we are investigating insofar as it has a relation to the body. But in itself, that entity (which we may as well keep calling 'soul') does not need to have any such relation. Its connection to the body and operation of the bodily powers is accidental to it. Thus Aristotle's attempted definition is more like a nominal description of the soul. It would be like trying to define 'wolf' and coming up with 'the cause of terrified flight among sheep'. Wolves really do cause that to happen, just as the soul really does perfect the body; but in neither case is it a good definition.

At the end of this chapter Ibn Sīnā makes a first attempt at conveying the true nature of the soul with his famous 'flying man' thought experiment. We'll come back to that in the next section. For now let's page forward to the fifth part of the treatise on the soul, where he gives his main proof of the human soul's incorporeality. This takes its departure point from our capacity to grasp intelligible forms. If the power to do this were seated in a bodily organ, then the form would be received in the parts of that organ and thus divided, the way that colour is spread out across parts of a surface when the surface takes on the colour. More generally, as already we know, intellection requires abstracting the form from its material accoutrements, like place and divisibility. It would undo this process if the intelligible form were simply received in a new matter, effectively adding back to the form precisely the extrinsic features that had to be removed in order to grasp it as an intelligible.

Ibn Sīnā clearly sees this as an original contribution which improves on Aristotle's proof that the intellect uses no bodily organ. This traded on the idea that intellect is potentially all forms and thus cannot itself have any actual formal properties, which it would have if it were in an organ. Suppose for example that the intellect were seated in the heart, which is hot: then the intellect would not be potentially 'hot', ready to receive the form of heat as an intelligible object, but already actually hot. Ibn Sīnā's argument does have in common with this proof of Aristotle's that it moves from the function of intellect to its ontological nature. This is itself a by-product of Ibn Sīnā's faculty-based approach to psychology. Since we grasp the intellect in the first instance as a power for performing a certain kind of activity, we can only show what kind of entity it is—namely, an immaterial substance—by working backwards from the nature of that activity. In turn, the nature of the activity is inferred from the nature of the object grasped by the intellect. Ultimately, it is the indivisibility of the intelligible object that underwrites the proof, since we argue from this to the indivisibility and hence incorporeality of the mind.

How convincing is his argument? One potential weakness, pointed out by later critics including al-Ghazālī and Fakhr al-Dīn al Rāzī, is that it seems to presuppose that a putative body in which the intellect might reside must be divisible. Certainly that would be true if the intellect were seated in, say, the brain—Ibn Sīnā's own theory of the internal senses draws attention to the fact that it has several ventricles, and these can be divided further, as by a surgeon. But what if the intellect's seat were an atom, that is, an indivisible body? Then it could receive the intelligible form without the form's being divided. Not a bad point, but it ignores that Ibn Sīnā has argued separately against atomism, including in this very same chapter of *The Healing*. So all this line of critique really achieves is the caveat that Ibn Sīnā's proof of the human soul's incorporeality is only as strong as his refutation of atomism. A more telling and fundamental objection might question whether intellectual knowledge should really be understood as the 'reception of form'. If we instead think of knowledge as a *relation*, as was standardly done in *kalām*, then we would not need to worry that the object of intellection would need be divided. A divisible organ could be suitably related to an indivisible object, as when you use your brain to grasp the number four.

The flying man and self-awareness

Let's now retrace our steps and go back to the end of the first chapter of the psychology in *The Healing*, where Ibn Sīnā sets out the flying man thought experiment. Actually this is only one of several passages where he mentions it, with evident pride. The different texts have potentially important variations. For instance sometimes Ibn Sīnā asks us to suggest a person being created by God in mid-air, whereas elsewhere he asks the reader to imagine themselves created in that situation. But passing over these subtleties, here is the basic idea: God creates someone in mid-air. Out of deference to tradition I will call this person the 'flying man' even though the person is not really flying and doesn't need to be male.

The flying man is 'perfect' in the sense of being a mature adult with functioning powers, but he has only just been created, so has no memory of any sensory experiences. Furthermore, his sight is veiled and there is nothing to hear, smell, or taste; his limbs and fingers are splayed out so that he is not in contact with his own body. This is the reason he needs to be in mid-air, by the way: to stop him from touching the ground and having sensory input as a result. So what we have here is someone who is getting no input from his senses and has never had any input from the senses. Nor has he had opportunity to use *wahm* or imagination, since these require encounter with sensible particulars. Ibn Sīnā thus claims that the flying man will be unaware that he has a body, or even that there are such things as bodies. Yet—here comes the crucial move—the flying man is aware of the existence of his own 'self' (*dhāt*). But if he is aware of his self, and not aware of his body, then his self is evidently not the same as his body. Thus his self is incorporeal. As Ibn Sīnā says at the end of a later passage reprising the flying man, our bodily organs are like clothes that our soul or true self (*nafs*) can strip off.

Ibn Sīnā's satisfaction with this thought experiment is well justified, even if we don't conclude in the end that it works as he would like it to. The thought experiment can be stated quickly and in my experience tends to elicit enthusiastic debate. As with all philosophical thought experiments, the first reaction it tends to get is a stubborn refusal to engage with it, by questioning the set-up. Wouldn't the flying man be able to feel his heart beat, or have 'proprioception', which is your capacity to sense where your limbs are in space? Then he would know he had a body after all. Which is not wrong, but easily answered. God has just gone to the lengths of creating this man in mid-air, and could surely also block his proprioception too, or do whatever else is necessary to achieve genuine sensory deprivation.

A second response would be simply to reject Ibn Sīnā's claim that the flying man would have knowledge of the existence of his self. Maybe he cannot know he exists until he enjoys some sort of sensory input; this is what a thoroughgoing empiricist might say. Now, Ibn Sīnā does expect you to agree with him about this instinctively. He thinks it's just obvious that the flying man would know he exists. But if you don't agree, then he will not necessarily have to concede that there is an irresolvable clash of intuitions. Instead, he might refer you to his more general treatment of self-awareness. This topic is explored with particular nuance in his *Notes* and *Discussions*, because it was evidently a matter of some interest to his students who prompted the exchanges recorded in these works. But the way is prepared already in *The Healing*, where Ibn Sīnā argues that in addition to our various psychological faculties, there must be some 'single thing' with which the faculties are conjoined. This is 'that which each of us sees as himself'. The fact that the faculties have a unified underlying subject explains why they can interfere with one another. When a noise distracts you from thinking, it is because the attention of your 'self' is pulled from one kind of cognition to another. And as Ibn Sīnā says, whenever you do anything, you can say 'it is I who did this'. So the self explains our first-person perspective on the world.

The self is also aware of itself, and 'essentially' so, or so Ibn Sīnā claims in the *Notes*. Note that self-awareness is different from being aware of, say, the wolf you see crouching in front of you. It is eyesight that is directed at the wolf. Self-awareness is instead directed at the fact that it is you who is seeing the wolf using your eyesight. It seems that for Ibn Sīnā there can also be 'primitive' self-awareness, where one is simply aware of oneself without being aware of any cognitive activity or any object of a cognitive activity. This is why the flying man is able to know that he exists. In fact all of us are, according to Ibn Sīnā, *constantly* self-aware. As recorded in the *Discussions*, his foe Abū l-Qāsim al-Kirmānī questioned this claim by giving the example of people who are fast asleep. To which Ibn Sīnā replied that we are indeed aware of ourselves through the night while sleeping, it is just that we don't remember it. 'The awareness of self-awareness', he points out, 'is different from self-awareness.'

As this shows, Ibn Sīnā is not claiming that we go through life being explicitly aware of ourselves at all times: 'here I am seeing a wolf . . . here I am running in terror . . .' To the contrary, self-awareness is usually 'potential', as he puts it. We might rather say 'tacit'. As a couple of modern-day scholars have suggested, the tacit self-awareness underlying all our cognitive activity might be compared to our constant deployment of logical principles such as the law of non-contradiction. Everyone presupposes all the time, whenever they are reasoning, that the two sides of a contradiction cannot both be true, but only people who study logic ever make this explicit to themselves. Likewise it takes some effort, a directing of attention, to notice that we can be and in fact tacitly *are* constantly aware of ourselves. This may be why Ibn Sīnā calls the flying man case a *tanbīh*, meaning 'reminder' or 'admonition'. It alerts you to your own immediate access to your self, and the fact that this access does not require your body.

Which brings us to a further possible objection to the flying man passage. At the crucial stage of the argument, we saw Ibn Sīnā saying that if the flying man is aware of his self, but not his body, then his self cannot be his body. He states the principle underlying this inference: 'you know that what is affirmed is distinct from what is not affirmed'. Sadly, this principle is false. To use a standard example, which as it happens also involves a flying man, Lois might be aware that Clark Kent is at the *Daily Planet* without being aware that Superman is there, since Lois doesn't know his secret identity. But this wouldn't mean that Clark Kent is not Superman. Similarly, Ibn Sīnā's flying man might be aware of his self without being aware of his body, simply because he doesn't have any way to learn that his self really is his body.

A number of solutions have been proposed to this difficulty. Here is one, which I have endorsed elsewhere. Think back to the context of the flying man passage. Ibn Sīnā has just been critiquing the Aristotelian definition of soul, on the grounds that it picks out the soul only through its accidental connection to the body. As he says at the start of the passage with the thought experiment, he wants to give us a way to grasp what the soul is in its essence (*māhiyya*), or rather what it is *not*. In terms of the logical system discussed in Chapter 2, he wants to show us that it is not a 'constituent' of the soul's essence to be corporeal or have any connection to body. And the thought experiment does show this, because the flying man is able to *know* that he exists without knowing that his body, or indeed any body, exists. But you cannot properly know that something exists if you are unaware whether one of its essential constituents has been satisfied. The interpretation just sketched gains some support from noting that the Arabic word I've been translating as 'self', *dhāt*, can also be translated as 'essence', and has meant this previously throughout the chapter. Thus the flying man would actually be grasping his *essence* through self-awareness, and grasping that his essence has existence. Given that he is oblivious of bodies, he could not do this if it were essential to the soul that it be connected to body.

Let us now pose a final question about self-awareness: how does it fit into Ibn Sīnā's faculty psychology? It may seem obvious that it is not any one faculty that is responsible for our self-awareness, because that awareness is meant to underlie the activities of all the faculties. Whether I see a wolf, imagine a wolf, or think about the essential nature of wolves, I can think 'it is I who did that'. But in the *Discussions*, Ibn Sīnā at least toys with the idea that it is really the intellect that is self-aware. This looks at first to be ruled out by the fact that each of us is a particular, or individual, whereas the intellect thinks about universal intelligibles. Ibn Sīnā here observes, however, that what impedes intellection is not particularity as such, but materiality or corporeality. Remember that the problem was features like divisibility that come along with matter. So if the self is immaterial, maybe it could be grasped by the intellect after all.

In fact Ibn Sīnā seems to be torn between two ideas about the self. On the one hand, following a broadly Platonic tradition, he thinks that each person is ultimately the substance that he identifies with the rational soul or intellect. As he says in the *Pointers*, 'it just *is* you'. Lower capacities and faculties are only 'branches' from this true self. On the other hand, Ibn Sīnā also has the more innovative idea that selfhood might be even more fundamental than intellect, because intellectual thinking is just one of many things the self can be aware of itself as doing. Following this idea, he says in the *Notes* that 'our awareness of ourselves is our very existence'. Later thinkers will exploit this tension and further develop the idea of a single subject of awareness, to the point that they question whether we need faculty psychology at all.

The afterlife

At the end of his *Incoherence of the Philosophers* al-Ghazālī condemns Ibn Sīnā—or rather the *falāsifa*, but we know who he means—for three teachings that constitute apostasy from Islam. One of them is the denial of the resurrection of the body. And from the foregoing it should be clear that Ibn Sīnā would, at best, have little use for a resurrected body. His proof that we can survive death turns on identifying a capacity of the soul that needs no bodily organ, and this is intellection. The intellect may be the true self, or alternatively, if the true self is awareness of oneself, then one could have that without needing to perform additional functions aside from intellection. In short, it looks like Ibn Sīnā's version of the afterlife would appeal only to a philosopher. It will be a continued existence involving nothing beyond pure intellectual activity.

There are a couple of difficulties here, though, one pragmatic and one of philosophical principle. The pragmatic problem is that Ibn Sīnā would quite like to say something in support of the idea that we are rewarded and punished after death, which is so important in Islamic belief. Towards this end he suggests that people with an unduly intense affection for their own bodies and bodily pleasures will be tormented after death by longing for what they have lost. So God doesn't actually have to do anything to punish bad people: they are punished by their own vicious desires. It must be said, though, that it is not so clear how a pure intellect could experience any of that. The difficulty of principle is that we need to guarantee that my soul after death is still me. This is what philosophers now call the 'problem of identity over time', which is not to be confused with the problem of individuation *at* a time, though Ibn Sīnā has things to say about that too. If what guarantees that my soul retains its identity across my life is a connection to *my* body rather than any other body, then how will my soul stay the same individual after I lose my body, perhaps through an unfortunate encounter with a wolf?

Individuation

Ibn Sīnā thinks we live in a world made up of particular individuals, which need to be grasped universally through an operation of the mind. But in respect of what are the particular things individuals in the first place? As Ibn Sīnā says, things that do not differ in respect of quiddity or form must still be distinguished somehow, to explain why they are not just identical. One possibility would be to appeal to the accidental features that belong to two members of the same species: for instance, this man is a philosopher, whereas that man is not, which differentiates them. But in the metaphysical section of *The Healing*, Ibn Sīnā rejects this strategy. We might provide a list of features, for example about Socrates: 'the righteous philosopher unjustly put to death in a given city on a given day'. Assuming no other righteous philosophers were executed on the same day in Athens, this would indeed pick out Socrates uniquely. But Ibn Sīnā thinks that is not enough. In theory there *could* have been another individual to whom all this applies (if Plato had nobly stepped forward to die with his master, perhaps), and this mere possibility means the combination of features does not individuate. That will be true no matter how long a list of features we devise.

So what would be enough? We need something that would be really unique, and it seems that Ibn Sīnā thought the best bet

(*continued*)

would be spatiotemporal location. No other object is in exactly the same places as Socrates at the same times, nor *could* any other object be there since things cannot overlap in space. Thus Ibn Sīnā says, when criticizing the theological claim that God will resurrect bodies that are identical to bodies that have long been destroyed, that this is impossible because the original bodies were individuated in part by the time at which they existed. Ibn Sīnā does not think that matter as such individuates, but matter plays a role because it accounts for the 'extraneous attachments' that attach to an essence and 'render it individual', as he says in the *Pointers*. This calls our attention to the fact that his strategy will not work for immaterial entities, which don't occupy specific places at specific times. Still, a soul might be individuated indirectly through its initial relationship to a spatiotemporally located body.

To this you might say, 'Ibn Sīnā is a dualist, so why would a connection to my body be responsible for the identity of my soul?' Well, remember that all natural substances, including humans, come to be when suitably prepared matter receives a form from the Active Intellect. Ibn Sīnā takes this point so seriously that he uses it in a refutation of the theory of metempsychosis, that is, the idea that a single soul can go from one body to another after death. This can be ruled out, because the new body will automatically get a *new* soul when it is prepared to receive one, so the reincarnated soul would find itself sharing the body with that new soul, which is absurd. Thus the soul's initial existence as an individual, at least, does seem to be due to the body. But once the soul has arrived, it may nonetheless not need the body to keep on being the soul that it is. Maybe it will be distinguished by the intellectual knowledge it has acquired and retained, or the character traits it has developed. Or maybe it will continue being the same entity because it is nothing but a self-aware subject who keeps being self-aware: this subjective, first-person perspective is not one that is shared with anyone else.

Chapter 4
Science

In the realm of natural philosophy, Ibn Sīnā covers more or less the territory surveyed by Aristotle, especially in *The Healing*, which has sections that correspond to the Aristotelian *Physics*, *On the Heavens*, *On Generation and Corruption*, and the *Meteorology*, as well as the spurious *On Plants*. In *The Healing* zoology is covered in a single book called *Animals*, but that was also truc of the Arabic translation of Aristotle's several treatises on the topic. This should not lead us to assume that Ibn Sīnā is content simply to repeat Aristotelian doctrine, though. He is aware of the late ancient commentary tradition and also of previous Arabic literature on natural philosophy, and thus offers novel defences against objections raised since Aristotle, while also adjusting the latter's teachings where he sees fit. An even more dramatic change is that he integrates Galenic medicine with Aristotelian natural philosophy, giving careful thought to the relationship between these two disciplines.

The cosmos

In antiquity, cosmologists had been divided over the question whether space is infinite or has a limit, with the Stoics and Epicureans adopting the former view and the Neoplatonists and Aristotelians the latter. Ibn Sīnā goes with the second option, and envisions the universe as a spherical cosmos beyond which there is nothing at all, not even void space. Almost the entirety of this cosmos is taken up with concentrically arranged spheres, which are rotating around a centre point. Upon these transparent spheres are seated the visible planets, whose motions allow for the astronomical study of the rotation of the spheres. Each of the spheres has a soul, which moves the sphere, and an intellect associated with that soul. So for Ibn Sīnā the study of ensouled things extends all the way to the edge of the universe: he even calls heaven an 'animal' or 'living being' (*ḥayawān*). Ultimately God is the explanation of this whole system, both because the series of celestial intellects descend from Him in an emanative chain, and because each celestial soul is causing motion out of the urge to imitate the eternal contemplation of its associated intellect, which in turn is contemplating God.

The celestial realm is for Ibn Sīnā perfect and, with the exception of the rotations of the spheres, unchanging. Nothing is ever generated or destroyed there. Things are different in the relatively small space around the centre point of the universe, which is where we find ourselves. Below the lowest sphere, that of the Moon, is the 'sublunary' realm where instead of ungenerable and indestructible matter, things are made of the four elements: air, earth, fire, and water. The forms of these elements, and of the more complex substances yielded when they combine, are bestowed by the lowest of the celestial intellects, the 'giver of forms' or 'Active Intellect' which we have met in previous chapters. This intellect is also the source of prime matter, a featureless substrate that underlies even the four rudimentary elements. In addition to form and matter, which are the 'internal' causes of a physical thing, Ibn Sīnā follows Aristotle in recognizing two other, 'external' kinds of cause, namely efficient (a source of existence, form, or motion) and final (a goal of change). Note that God is both the ultimate source of existence and ultimate goal of motion, so He is both an efficient and final cause for all things, though mostly indirectly. More on this in the next chapter.

Body and matter

Aristotle did not argue explicitly for the postulation of prime matter. In fact, many modern-day scholars question whether he even believed in it, though in antiquity and the medieval period this was taken for granted by all commentators. By contrast Ibn Sīnā devotes careful consideration to the relationship between body and matter, which for him are not to be identified with one another. (On this and other topics we're about to consider, he is especially responding to the critical discussions on Aristotle's *Physics* offered by the late ancient commentator John Philoponus.) For Ibn Sīnā body is defined as continuity (*ittiṣāl*), which means divisible extension. Body is that in which one can demarcate three directions or dimensions, like the three axes of a coordinate system. Body as such does not have to have any specific dimensions, since even a single body can vary in volume, as when something cools down and becomes more dense. But neither can body exist without having some given dimensions at any one time. This gives us a nice illustration of a logical contrast we discussed earlier: to be extended and divisible are 'constitutive' properties of body, but to have a certain determinate size is 'concomitant'.

Since body is for Ibn Sīnā so basic, just divisible extension, we might wonder why it is necessary also to posit prime matter. His answer comes in the form of a thought experiment. Since body is divisible, let's take a single body and divide it, here considering it just as a body, not as a body of any particular kind. It will clearly no longer be *the same* body, since it was just one body before and now it is two bodies. So something still more fundamental has undergone that change. This is matter, which does not even have extension in its own right and is therefore not divisible. Since matter is in itself free of all determination, Ibn Sīnā says that it is only a 'substrate' for various forms; a proper 'subject' by contrast would be an actual substance, such as a rock or animal (he thereby clears up a potential confusion between two senses of the Arabic word *mawḍūʿ*). Likewise body is only a 'second substrate', matter to which the form of divisible extension has been added.

By defining body as divisible Ibn Sīnā rules out the possibility of an *indivisible* body, which is not an innocent or uncontroversial move on his part. In fact the dominant theory of bodies among Muslim intellectuals was atomism, because almost all theologians adopted this theory, with many variations on points of detail. Unsurprisingly then, Ibn Sīnā is at pains to refute atomism. To understand his arguments we need to realize that *kalām* atoms were not those of ancient atomists like Democritus and Epicurus. They were not very small bodies which simply 'cannot be cut' (this being the etymology of 'atom') but point-like substances which 'occupy space', yet have no extension and thus no internal parts at all. To this Ibn Sīnā first rejoins that if the individual atoms have no extension, then when they are put together they will not form an extension either, however numerous they are (zero plus zero is still zero). Furthermore, we can perform another thought experiment. Line up three atoms A B C in a row so that they are touching. A will touch B on one side; C will touch B on the other side. But if B has two distinct sides, then it has two halves or parts and is extended after all. Alternatively both A and C might be touching 'all of' B, fully overlapping with it. But if that is true we're back to the problem that adding atoms to one another will never yield extension.

Now, obviously Ibn Sīnā does not think that one can *actually* divide, and sub-divide, and sub-sub-divide, any body indefinitely. Our ability to keep performing divisions is subject to practical constraints. But every body, no matter how small, is in principle subject to division. On the other hand, dividing beyond a certain 'minimum' will inevitably corrupt the form of the thing being divided. Here we have Ibn Sīnā's theory of 'natural minimums'. A substance like water has a smallest possible size, and if a particle of that size is divided it will no longer be water. Of course it will have to be some other kind of substance instead: you can't just have pure matter or pure body floating around, even at minuscule sizes. What we should imagine is that the particle of water is destroyed and the matter absorbed into some larger mass that has overwhelmed it, like air.

Time and place

Ibn Sīnā designates physics as the science that studies natural bodies insofar as they are subject to alteration (*taghayyur*). This means that for him, as for Aristotle, this discipline must study those phenomena that belong to bodies insofar as they change and move. Prominent examples include time (*zamān*) and place (*makān*). To get us started in grasping what time is, Ibn Sīnā points out the phenomenon of differing spatial motions, for example two bodies starting and stopping together but travelling different distances, or travelling the same distance even though one starts before the other. We would probably capture his point by saying that velocity is a function of distance covered in a time. But thinking within an Aristotelian framework, he invokes a body's possibility (*imkān*) to, for instance, move over a certain distance either more or less quickly. So time is a 'size' of the motion just as much as the distance covered.

The reason this is a more Aristotelian way to think about the situation is that it ties time very strongly to bodies, via the motions that bodies perform. Like Aristotle, Ibn Sīnā thinks there would be no time if there were no bodies, or if bodies could never move. The reason we have temporal 'before and after' is that time measures motions which have their own priority, for example a motion from A to C is first at A, then at B, then at C. Time also measures changes other than spatial motion: the ripening of an apple, and not only the apple's fall from the tree. But Ibn Sīnā picks up on an idea found earlier in the Aristotelian tradition, especially in Alexander of Aphrodisias, though it was tentatively and briefly suggested by Aristotle himself. The idea is to associate time 'primarily' with just one particular motion, and only 'secondarily' with other motions. This favoured motion will be the fastest one in the whole universe, the daily rotation of the outermost heavenly sphere, which accounts for the apparent motion of the fixed stars around us once each day. In reality of course it is the Earth that is spinning once per day. But we are in a pre-Copernican world here, so Ibn Sīnā assumes it is the heavens going around us and not us rotating below the heavens. The advantage of this is that we have a single, continuous motion which supplies a universal framework for all other change. So we could say for example that the apple *first* ripened, and *then* fell from the tree, because these distinct changes happen during different phases of the continuous heavenly rotation. Furthermore time will already have been going on before any change occurs, since the heavenly rotation is eternal. Time does not begin, nor will it end, because it is dependent on the everlasting motion of an ungenerated and indestructible celestial body.

This puts Ibn Sīnā at odds with a rival theory of time, inspired by Plato, that had been adopted by Abū Bakr al-Rāzī and would later be defended by Fakhr al-Dīn al-Rāzī, according to which time is not dependent on bodies—in fact doubly dependent, on Ibn Sīnā's view, since it is the extension of the motion which in turn depends on bodies. Instead the two Rāzīs thought that time subsists in its own right, and makes it possible for there to be priority in change, instead of vice versa. One powerful argument given by the later al-Rāzī was that, Ibn Sīnā's preference for the celestial sphere's motion notwithstanding, every motion considered just as a motion should have its own temporal magnitude. (Notice that this premise is based on Ibn Sīnā's own conceptual apparatus: time is a concomitant of motion *as such*, so it makes no difference which motion we are considering. A small example of how Ibn Sīnā's successors used his own techniques against him.) If then we have two motions going on at once, then we are forced to say that there are two times unfolding 'at the same time', giving us a second-order time—a time at which other times are occurring—which looks absurd in itself and would also threaten to start an infinite regress of ever higher-order times.

As for place, on Ibn Sīnā's view it is like time in being dependent on bodies. He endorses the Aristotelian definition: the place of each body is the surface of the body or bodies directly in contact with it from the outside. For example the place of a fish floating in the sea is the interior surface of the seawater where the water is in contact with the fish. While this may seem strange, Ibn Sīnā asserts that it actually fits better with our intuitions than rival definitions, for instance a *kalām* account that makes the place of something the surface it is sitting (or 'placed') upon, so that the coaster would be the 'place' of the glass. Ibn Sīnā doesn't like this idea, since he thinks it is obvious that a place should fully contain what is in it.

The more innovative aspects of Ibn Sīnā's discussion of place have to do with his refutation of objections to the Aristotelian definition. I'll consider two. First, as already pointed out in antiquity, according to this definition the universe itself has no place. Remember, there is nothing at all outside the cosmos, and certainly no further body surrounding it. Various attempts had been made to dodge this argumentative bullet, but Ibn Sīnā elects simply to bite it: the outermost sphere indeed has no place. How can that be, since it is rotating and thus engaging in spatial motion, which seems like it should count as change *in respect of place*? Ibn Sīnā's answer is that the rotation is change in position, not place, since the parts of the sphere are changing their position relative to the poles of the sphere, that is, the points at the end of the axis of rotation.

The second objection also has to do with the idea that spatial motion is change of place. Imagine again our fish in the sea, but now add that the water around it is flowing. Bizarrely, it now seems we have to say that the fish is moving, even if it is sitting still, because the surface around it is its place, and this surface is changing all the time. Again Ibn Sīnā bites the bullet: the place of the fish is indeed changing. But it would be a mistake to infer from this that the fish is moving, because to move is to have a 'principle of change'. It's another clever response, which reminds us that within Aristotelianism motion or change is fundamentally an activity undertaken or undergone by that which moves or changes, and not a phenomenon defined relative to some external context.

A last question about place brings Ibn Sīnā, yet again, into conflict with *kalām*. Like ancient atomists, the theologians thought that space can be either occupied by a body (in the first instance, by an atom) or not occupied by a body, in which case we can speak of empty space or 'void' (*khalā'*). By contrast Ibn Sīnā really has no use for the notion of 'space'. There are only bodies with magnitudes and (except in the case of the outermost sphere) surrounding bodies that provide them with their places. His most impressive argument against space, to my mind, turns on an idea we've already encountered more than once, namely the need for any two things that are not identical to have different features that individuate them. If we have a stretch of space that is occupied by a body, then the extension of that region of space will be exactly the same as the extension of the body. Suppose the body is a cube, for example. Then the space it is occupying will also be shaped like a cube of the same dimensions. But, says Ibn Sīnā, there is nothing to distinguish these two extensions from one another. Thus we cannot say that the extension of the body and the spatial extension are non-identical. And since the body clearly does have an extension, the one we should dispense with is the spatial extension.

Medicine and biology

Let's now change tack a bit and look at a more concrete dimension of Ibn Sīnā's natural philosophy, namely his work on medicine. Or rather his works on medicine, which are numerous. Pride of place must go to the *Canon of Medicine* (*Qānūn fī l-Ṭibb*) (Figure 4), which does for this discipline more or less what *The Healing* does for philosophy, but with Galen as the central authority rather than

4. **Manuscript of Ibn Sīnā's major medical treatise, the *Qānūn*.**

Aristotle. There are also a much-read *Poem on Medicine* and a treatise on cardiac drugs, as well as an array of minor works on topics like urine, bloodletting, sexual intercourse, and the disease that would cause Ibn Sīnā's own demise, colic. In the *Autobiography* he remarks disarmingly that medicine is not a difficult discipline, so that he was able to 'excel in it after a very short period of time, so that excellent physicians began to study under me'. Part of the explanation here may be that medical study involves lots of brute force memorization, which came easily to Ibn Sīnā. But there is more to say about the method of medicine.

Here the first thing to sort out is how medicine is related to the more general concerns of natural philosophy dealt with in this chapter so far. It might seem that this relation must be loose, at best. How would knowing about cosmology, elemental theory, and so on help us treat patients? That question is implicitly answered at the beginning of the *Canon*, where Ibn Sīnā warns doctors against exploring the fundamental teachings of natural philosophy, not because they are irrelevant but because the physician should simply take them for granted. Thus in medicine one does not *prove* that there are four elements or four bodily humours that arise from them, but the doctor certainly needs to *accept* this, as so much therapy involves redressing imbalances in the humours. In other cases natural philosophy may establish truths the doctor can simply ignore. For instance in medicine we don't need to know whether the soul is one, whether the different organs instead have different individual souls, or for that matter how to define time and place. The doctor should know about the internal senses but can get by with recognizing only three out of the five, since his goal of treating disease does not require him to distinguish between the two kinds of memory or to know at all about the estimative power.

In short, medicine is 'subordinated' to natural philosophy in the way discussed in Chapter 2. Whereas natural philosophy studies all sensible bodies, medicine studies only human bodies, and these only insofar as they are subject to health and sickness. Thus Ibn Sīnā describes medicine as a 'derivative' (*farʿī*) science, that is, one that relates to natural philosophy as a 'branch' (*farʿ*) does to a root. Yet medicine does have scientific ambitions. In the opening of the *Canon* Ibn Sīnā says it should pursue 'demonstrative proofs' concerning diseases, their causes and symptoms, and also the restoration and preservation of health. He has interesting things to say about how this is achieved. Since the underlying causes of disease and health are not 'manifest' they need to be grasped indirectly, inferring those causes on the basis of sensory experience. For this task Ibn Sīnā recommends the method of experience as opposed to mere induction. He refers to this in the *Autobiography* when he says that through his medical explorations he learned about many therapies 'that can be acquired only through experience'.

Vision

Among the achievements of Islamic science is the great progress that was made in understanding the mechanism of vision. This is typically, and not without reason, credited to Ibn Sīnā's contemporary Ibn al-Haytham, who was influential on European science under his Latinized name Alhazen. But in fact Ibn Sīnā had a very similar theory. The tradition down to their time saw a contest between two models for explaining vision, 'intromissionist' and 'extramissionist'. As the names convey, an intromissionist theory explains vision in terms of something coming *into* the eye, as in Aristotle's theory, which has visual forms transmitted from the object to the viewer by means of an illuminated transparent medium, usually air. In an extramissionist theory, something instead goes *out of* the eye: a 'visual ray'. This view goes back to Plato and Galen, with the latter saying that the visual ray is made of 'spirit' or *pneuma*, the same subtle body that vivifies the whole human or animal body. The visual ray theory was allied to the ideas of figures like Euclid and Ptolemy, who used geometry to represent vision and to explain phenomena like perspective and mirror reflection. In the Islamic world, al-Kindī had pursued this sort of account, according to which lines drawn from the eye to the visual object in a geometrical diagram represent visual rays coming from the eye in physical reality.

Ibn Sīnā and Ibn al-Haytham resolve the impasse by accepting an intromissionist theory but keeping the geometrical analysis. Indeed Ibn Sīnā says that this topic stands at the intersection of natural philosophy and geometry. There is a cone-shaped visual field, but this cone consists of coloured light coming from the object rather than of rays coming from the eye. The angle of the vertex of the cone, which is at the eye, dictates how large the object will appear. Aristotle is right to say that a visual 'image' is

(*continued*)

transmitted to the eye, but in a departure from the Aristotelian account, Ibn Sīnā denies that the medium needs to be illuminated. It just needs not to obstruct the coloured light coming from the visual object, as an opaque body would do. By contrast the coloured surface *does* need to be illuminated, which Ibn Sīnā describes as actualizing the colour to make it visible. The upshot is an explanation of vision that is much closer to being correct than either of the rival theories that had come down to him through the Greek and Arabic literature on optics.

In this respect medicine bears similarities to another science, zoology. The study of animals frequently involves inferences about imperceptible causes, for example organs that are too small to see. The zoologist should, again, use 'experience' to do this. A nice example is Ibn Sīnā's way of establishing that fish must have auditory and olfactory organs. He has himself observed the way that they flee from loud noises and seem to appreciate music, and also mentions how fishermen have learned to use milk in water as a kind of bait to trap them. Thus we have a proof that fish can hear and smell, a proof that goes beyond mere probability. Through such means the zoologist is able to achieve scientific classification of the animal world, attending to differences in habitat, food, character (*akhlāq*, a word also used of human ethical traits), activities, and parts. The zoologist also studies cross-species phenomena like (external) sensation, voluntary motion, sleep, and sexual difference.

His methodological commitment to careful observation notwithstanding, Ibn Sīnā has the reputation for being a brilliant and influential theorist of medicine, rather than a practitioner. This is not entirely wrong. Ibn Sīnā's *Canon* does provide the theoretical basis for the discipline of medicine, including what he calls the 'theory of practice', that is, general truths that one would

Experience (*tajriba*)

Already in antiquity medical literature had been an arena for disputes about scientific method. Galen talked about the rival approaches of 'rationalist' and 'empiricist' doctors, the former trying to devise causal theories to underpin their therapeutic practice, the latter simply keeping track of what seems to work and repeating successful treatments. Galen was scornful of the empiricists, but admitted the need to bring experience to bear when developing theories. Ibn Sīnā agrees with this and develops the idea into a full-blown theory of scientific method. He contrasts 'experience' (*tajriba*) with 'induction' (*istiqrā'*). The difference is that induction simply generalizes from observed phenomena, for instance by assuming that if applying a cold compress to a rash worked in one case, it should work for other cases too. Ibn Sīnā critiques this approach with an example that is not original with him: using induction, someone from Africa might conclude that all humans have black skin, since everyone this person has ever met has been black. By contrast *tajriba*, sometimes translated 'methodic experience', takes more care to make repeated observations under similar circumstances, makes inferences to underlying causes, and recognizes the limits of the conclusions that can be drawn. Tellingly, Ibn Sīnā illustrates with an example drawn from medicine, namely the effect of scammony, a plant which causes purgation. Experiences of scammony allow us to postulate a purgative power in this natural substance, but with caveats. For instance, scammony growing in some other part of the world may not have the same effect, and the conditions of an individual body or the body's environment may affect the working of the scammony.

need to know as a practitioner. Since medieval medicine was so oriented around book-learning, the task of assembling the *Canon* was mostly a matter of systematically presenting the teachings of Galen and other authors, and of adjudicating disputes that had arisen in the tradition. Perhaps the most obvious of these was the question of which organ is primary in the human body: the heart, as claimed by Aristotle, or the brain, as claimed by Galen? Ibn Sīnā took a nuanced view on this question. As we know he located numerous cognitive faculties, of both humans and animals, in the brain. But for him the heart is the source of spirit (*rūḥ*, translating Greek *pneuma*), which is the vehicle for life in the body as a whole. Thus the heart is the seat of the 'vital faculty', a fundamental concept in medicine, and also of the emotions.

Despite his theoretical focus, it would do Ibn Sīnā a disservice to say that he never practised medicine. The *Autobiography* claims that he acquired patrons on the strength of his expertise as a doctor, and it has been shown that his *Canon* and other medical writings frequently allude to his own hands-on experience. He states repeatedly that he has 'tested' or 'tried' (*jarrada*) various remedies and drugs, as well as dietary measures to preserve health: he warmly recommends camel milk, advice I am unfortunately unable to confirm. It might be said, then, that with him the situation is the reverse of his predecessor Abū Bakr al-Rāzī (see Chapter 1), the only figure who can rival his pre-eminence in the history of Islamic medicine. Due to his documented work in hospitals and his massive collection of medical notes *The Comprehensive Book* (*al-Ḥāwī*), al-Rāzī is often cast in the role of practitioner *par excellence*. But, while that work does present information from al-Rāzī's own experiences, it is for the most part a record of his reading in Galenic and Hippocratic medicine. So he was in fact a professionally active doctor with extensive theoretical interests. Conversely Ibn Sīnā was primarily a theoretician, so his reputation to this effect is not misleading. Yet he did treat patients and learned from doing so, in precisely the way recommended by his own epistemology.

Chapter 5
God and the world

As I've already said and will be explaining in more detail in the next chapter, Ibn Sīnā's impact on subsequent philosophy in the Islamic world was pervasive and made itself felt in many areas. But if you had to choose just one idea as his most influential, it would probably be his proof for the existence of God. He argues that there is exactly one being in the world that by its own nature cannot fail to exist. This is the 'necessary existent' (*wājib al-wujūd*), which comes to be something of a new designation for God in later philosophical writing, almost like a proper name. While the proof was widely admired, Ibn Sīnā was frequently criticized for trying to derive all claims about God from the concept of necessity. In an anticipation of the medieval 'voluntarism' that emerged still later in Latin scholasticism, the critics argued for replacing Ibn Sīnā's necessitarian God with one who does *exist* necessarily, as he had argued, but *chooses* voluntarily between alternative possibilities, something he had denied.

Essence and existence

Before we can get into the proof, we need first to acquaint ourselves with a distinction that is fundamental to Ibn Sīnā's metaphysics: between essence and existence. At one level the distinction is simple enough. It just means that there is a difference between what something is (by its very nature, not accidentally) and whether it exists, or as we might say using more technical language, whether the essence is instantiated. But there is a lot more that can be said about it. A good approach is to look at the historical background that led Ibn Sīnā to his insight. The distinction is foreshadowed in Aristotle, who in his *Posterior Analytics* likewise contrasted the question what something is (*ti esti*) with the question whether it is (*ei esti*). But this was really an epistemic contrast, between two sorts of inquiry one might undertake. Ibn Sīnā's distinction is instead properly metaphysical, and implies among other things that existence needs to be *given* to an essence in order that the essence be instantiated.

For this we need to look again at the history of *kalām*. Members of the Muʿtazilite school were known for asserting the apparently paradoxical claim that the 'non-existent' (*al-maʿdūm*) is a 'thing' (*shayʾ*). They had in mind passages in the Quran such as 'when God wills a thing (*shayʾ*) He says to it, "Be!" and it is' (36:82). This suggests that whatever God wishes to create is already a 'thing' before God creates it. Philosophically too, it makes sense that God cannot direct His will or knowledge at what He intends to create, if it is not 'something'. Furthermore, non-existents seem already to have certain features *before* they exist, features that distinguish them from one another. An as-yet-non-existing sheep is herbivorous, whereas an as-yet-non-existing wolf is carnivorous. This presupposes that they have some kind of reality (*thubūt*), since one cannot ascribe properties to something that is in no way real. So these non-existents must be 'things'.

Here then we have the intuition underlying Ibn Sīnā's distinction, that a thing's essential features are independent of whether or not that thing exists. As if in confirmation that *kalām* is indeed in the background here, Ibn Sīnā even uses the neologism 'thing-ness' (*shayʾiyya*) as a synonym for essence. His position is so close to that of the Muʿtazilites, in fact, that later authors like Fakhr al-Dīn al-Rāzī will sometimes describe him as a partisan of that school's view. But from another angle, Ibn Sīnā could seem to be agreeing with the Mu‘tazilites’ opponents, the Ash‘arites. They said that reality consists exclusively of what God has in fact created. Talk of what God *could* create, *intends* to create, or *knows* He could create is just talk about God’s power, will, and wisdom. It is not about real things that are somehow independent of Him, like switches waiting to be turned from ‘off’ to ‘on’ by divine fiat. And like the Ash‘arites, Ibn Sīnā says that there are no non-existing things. Or to put it another way, that every possible thing receives existence.

On the face of it, this seems a ridiculous thing to say. What about centaurs and leprechauns, or the sister my parents never produced for me? It seems obvious that they could exist, but do not. Ibn Sīnā considers similar examples, such as the seven-sided house: one might build such a thing, but perhaps no one ever has. Yet the very fact that we are indeed *considering* these things shows that they do have existence after all. It is just that they exist in the mind (*fī l-dhihn*), not in extramental, concrete reality (*fī l-a‘yān* or *fī l-khārij*). As Ibn Sīnā says in the metaphysics of *The Healing*, even if we only make a negative judgement about something, it has to at least ‘have a form in the mind’. Once we add that things can exist mentally as well as concretely, we can say that every essence has existence of one sort or another. This allows him to have the best of both *kalām* views. Like the Mu‘tazilites he is able to say that things have their essential properties independently of their existence; like the Ash‘arites he does not have to postulate some sort of ‘reality’ for things that don’t exist, since there aren’t any.

At this point, you might wonder why it is so important to distinguish essence from existence, if all essences have existence anyway. One reason has to do with causation. Since essential properties are indeed independent of existence, no cause is needed to account for them. An example from Ibn Sīnā’s *Book of Knowledge* is that nothing needs to make black be a colour. Black just is a colour, all on its own. By contrast, a cause is needed to make black exist, because there is nothing about blackness that guarantees its existence. Going just by its essence, it might exist, or it might not. So something else must come along and bestow existence upon the essence, either by thinking about it so as to give it mental existence, or by making it exist in concrete reality.

Later in the tradition, this was often expressed using the language of 'preponderance' (*tarjīḥ*). Something needs to tip the scales, as it were, in favour of blackness existing rather than not existing. You might remember my saying in Chapter 2 that according to Ibn Sīnā we have an immediate grasp of the 'modal' properties necessity, contingency, and impossibility. This is what 'contingency' means: a thing is contingent (*mumkin*) if its essence does not guarantee its own existence. Of course, the contingent thing's essence also does not guarantee its own *non*-existence, the way that something like a round square would do. The very nature of the round square (insofar as it has one) rules out that it exists, so no cause is required to explain its failing to exist. What about the reverse case, an essence that by its very nature cannot *fail* to exist? Something that exists without being caused to do so, the way that black is a colour all on its own? Is there any such thing?

The demonstration of the truthful

Ibn Sīnā thought that there is, and that he could prove it. This will of course be the 'necessary existent', also known as God. His argument for it received the rare distinction of having its own honorific, *burhān al-ṣiddiqīn*, meaning 'the demonstration of the truthful'. It deserves that honour, because it offered a genuine departure from arguments for the existence of God that had been given earlier in the history of philosophy. In particular, Ibn Sīnā was well aware that his approach differed from that of Aristotle. In the *Physics*, Aristotle had argued that since the heavenly motions are eternal, an infinite power is required to generate them. God is this infinite mover. As mentioned in passing already, Ibn Sīnā found this disappointing, since for him God should be established as a cause of existence and not just motion. So in *The Healing*, where he takes unusual care to engage with the Aristotelian tradition, he instead takes inspiration from Aristotle's *Metaphysics* book α (not book Λ, the *locus classicus* for Aristotle's conception of God) to present arguments for a first cause based on the idea of avoiding infinite causal regresses, and not only for the sake of explaining motion.

It is in other texts, like the *Salvation* and *Pointers*, that he presents his own, distinctive proof. It takes its departure from the fact that 'there is existence'. As we know by our primary concepts, existence can be either contingent or necessary. We want to show that there is in fact something necessarily existent, or put otherwise, that not all existents are contingent. Now, we've already seen that a contingent thing will not have existence through itself. Instead, it needs a cause to bestow existence upon it. Of course this cause need not be a necessary existent. It might just be another contingent thing, which was in turn caused to exist by some further contingent thing, and so on. Imagine a daughter caused by her mother, who is caused by the grandmother, who is caused by the great-grandmother, and so on. Indeed, this is a scenario Ibn Sīnā cannot rule out, since as we'll see below he thought that the universe is eternal and that there have always been humans. So there will be mothers and grandmothers all the way back into the infinite past.

Instead, he invites us to consider the whole set or 'aggregate' of contingent things. Presumably it too needs a cause, because the aggregate of contingent things will itself be contingent. Even if someone denies this, they will have to say that the aggregate is a *necessary* existent. But they would thereby concede what Ibn Sīnā is trying to prove, namely that something exists necessarily. So the opponent must admit that the aggregate is contingent, and thus that its existence must have a cause. What might that cause be? Perhaps one of the contingent items inside the aggregate. But then what makes that item exist? Ibn Sīnā argues that nothing can cause itself to exist. So it would have to be caused to exist by something else within the rest of the aggregate, which it is supposedly causing. That would mean that we have circular causation, but this too is absurd, argues Ibn Sīnā. Besides, what would entitle one contingent thing to be the cause of all the others? The only possibility Ibn Sīnā sees as viable, then, is that the cause of the contingent things is *outside* the aggregate of all contingent things. This will of course be a necessary thing, since it is not one of the contingents. QED.

One strength of Ibn Sīnā's proof is that it exploits an intuition that really does motivate many people to believe in God: there must be some reason why all this (gesticulating at the universe) exists! Ibn Sīnā ratifies that intuition, and argues that we can only explain the existence of contingent things, which in themselves have no claim to existence, by postulating a necessary cause. This way of seeing the proof takes it to be a kind of 'cosmological' argument, that is, one that proceeds from the fact of the universe's existence to a divine cause. But the proof has also been classified as an 'ontological' argument, meaning one that derives the existence of God from pure conceptual analysis. Then it would be like the famous proof offered by the somewhat later medieval Christian philosopher Anselm, which aims to establish God on the grounds that it would be self-contradictory to say that God, 'that than which nothing greater can be conceived', is non-existent.

This interpretive question, whether Ibn Sīnā's proof is cosmological or ontological, comes down to our reading of the opening premise, 'there is existence'. Does Ibn Sīnā mean by this that there are some things that factually exist, for instance you or me? Or does he only appeal to our primary concept of existence, and our conviction that there *can* be at least contingent existence? The proof might be thought to work on that basis. Not because, à la Anselm, it would be contradictory to claim that a necessary existent does not exist. If this were Ibn Sīnā's reasoning he would not need to bother with all that business about the aggregate of contingent things. Rather, because if there were no necessary existent, then contingent things could not exist after all, since there would be nothing to cause them. But that looks like a rather fishy line of argument, since the contingent things would be rendered impossible only extrinsically, by a lack of any cause. They would remain intrinsically contingent (and thus 'possible') by their own essences. In any case it is far easier to assume, as the cosmological reading would have it, that Ibn Sīnā argues from the factual existence of at least one contingent thing. After all, this is hardly a controversial starting point.

Now for a more fundamental question: does the proof work? One might protest at his move of lumping together all contingent things as an aggregate and asking what causes it. If each of the elements in the aggregate has been caused then why would we need to cause the whole aggregate in addition? After all every part of it has already been explained, and it is just a whole of these parts. To use our analogy, if each daughter has a mother back through the generations, then it is unclear why we would need a separate cause for the whole lineage. Another objection might be that there is a part–whole fallacy involved in saying that the aggregate of contingent things is itself contingent. Some properties transfer from part to whole: every drop of water is wet, and the whole bucketful of water is also wet. But some do not: every part of the clock is small, but the clock is big. But Ibn Sīnā already answered this move, when he said that if someone denies the contingency of the aggregate, they will have to say the aggregate is necessary. So the opponent has conceded what Ibn Sīnā is trying to prove: there is a necessary existent.

Another way to resist would have a similar outcome, at least in Ibn Sīnā's eyes. One could simply deny that contingent things always need external causes. Perhaps something contingent, the universe for instance, can exist just as a brute fact. True, it might not have existed, but here we are: the universe does exist, and we should resist the urge to explain it. If this objection were put to

Ibn Sīnā, I think he would either dismiss it as nonsensical or interpret it as the (for him, false) claim that the universe is in fact necessary, since by definition only a necessary existent can exist without a cause. He would then reiterate that this concedes the sought conclusion.

Here though, we come to an important limitation of the proof. To show that there is a necessary existent is not the same as proving that God exists. We still need to show that this necessary existent has the traits one would expect of the Abrahamic God: uniqueness, simplicity, immateriality, knowledge, omnipotence, benevolence, and so on. If the necessary existent is just the universe, as conceded by the opponent, then we have not proved the existence of God. Ibn Sīnā was however well aware of this, and duly provided further arguments to show that the necessary existent has these traits. Here we really do have a parallel with Anselm, who in his *Proslogion* first uses the 'that than which nothing greater can be conceived' formula to show that God exists (indeed, exists necessarily), and then goes on to extract a similar set of traits from the formula.

Necessitarianism

It's vital to see that this is the strategy of Ibn Sīnā's philosophical theology, since it helps to explain the aspect of that theology that would be most controversial in subsequent generations. He insists that everything about God is necessary, and he can hardly do otherwise, since necessity is his sole route into establishing truths about God. Ibn Sīnā would also add that there cannot be any contingent features in God anyway, because if there were, then some cause would be needed to bring these features about, and nothing exerts causal influence on God. Ibn Sīnā uses this premise, that God as a necessary being has no cause, to establish several important facts about Him, including His simplicity, His uniqueness, and His immateriality. After all, material causes are one of the four standard kinds of causal explanation in

Divine unity

The *shahāda*, or profession of Muslim faith, states that 'there is no God but God, and Muḥammad is His prophet'. Islamic theologians duly concerned themselves intensely with the oneness of God. Indeed the Muʿtazilites styled themselves as the 'upholders of unity and justice', the latter by insisting that humans act freely in order to safeguard God's justice in punishing and rewarding them, the former by denying any multiplicity of attributes in God. As this shows, the doctrine of God's unity (*tawḥīd*) can be interpreted not just as meaning that there is only one God, but also as meaning that God is simple. Ibn Sīnā argues that both points can be extracted from God's necessity, and in particular from His having no cause. God is simple, that is, has no parts, because parts count as a cause for the whole they constitute, as a piece of furniture is caused by the parts that are assembled to produce it. Of course the parts are not the *only* cause of the whole. There is also the increasingly frustrated person trying to follow the assembly directions. But they are still a cause in a sense. And if some further cause were needed to put God's putative parts together, then all the more would God's necessity be undermined.

The argument for God's being unique is somewhat more involved (I here consider the version found in his *Pointers*). If there were two necessary existents, Ibn Sīnā asks, what would distinguish them from one another? It cannot be something that follows just from being a necessary existent, because that would be a feature they share, given that they are both necessary existents. So it must be some feature that a necessary existent might have, or might lack. Let's say for the sake of argument that necessary existent 1 is red, and necessary existent 2 is blue. Then redness is a cause for 1, because it makes 1 distinct from 2; and the same goes for the blueness of 2. But 1 and 2 are both

(*continued*)

necessary existents, so they cannot have causes. Thus we cannot appeal to these extrinsic factors to distinguish them after all. Notice here how Ibn Sīnā again presupposes that two non-identical things must be differentiated by some property they do not share, an assumption we also saw in the context of his treatment of individuation (see Chapter 3) and his discussion of void (see Chapter 4).

Aristotelian philosophy, as we saw in the last chapter. So God cannot have any matter. By this simple bit of reasoning, we can now tie up a loose end: it is ruled out that the necessary existent is the universe itself, as it of course is a material entity.

Furthermore, Ibn Sīnā feels able to infer from God's immateriality that He is an intellect. This is because, as he puts it in *Pointers*, 'He subsists free from attachments, lacks, or materials . . . and what is like this grasps itself intellectually.' Here he is exploiting points made in his psychology, where he showed that human intellection is an immaterial activity and that things become intelligible for humans when they are freed from matter. Since God is immaterial, the only activity He can perform must likewise be intellection. And if He is immaterial then nothing prevents Him from being grasped intellectually, so He will be able to grasp Himself. Here we have a remarkable example of Ibn Sīnā's strategy for understanding the divine. He begins from the *negative* point that God has no cause, and moves from here to a *positive* characterization of God as a self-thinking intellect. Not coincidentally, that characterization echoes Aristotle's portrayal of God in his own *Metaphysics*. But it is reached in a completely new way.

Thus far many Muslim theologians would find little to object to. God exists necessarily, is simple and unique, has no body, and has knowledge? No disagreement there. But the theologians were less happy once they got into the details. Ibn Sīnā does believe that God has knowledge, but only of Himself. Or rather He does know other things, but indirectly, by grasping Himself as their ultimate cause. Notoriously, Ibn Sīnā claims that this will not allow God to grasp particulars 'as such'. Equally controversial is his view that His effects proceed from Him necessarily, and mostly indirectly. That they come forth from God necessarily should, at this point, come as no surprise. If His causing them to exist were contingent, then something would have to cause this contingency to be realized, compromising God's own necessity and freedom from causal influence.

That they come forth from Him mostly indirectly is due to another constraint, which came to be called the 'from one can come only one' rule, often known by its Latin tag, *ex uno non fit nisi unum*. Being simple, God can have only one effect. The same problem had been confronted by Plotinus and other late ancient Platonists, who were no less committed to the utter simplicity of their first principle, which they even called 'the One'. These Platonists always faced the difficulty of explaining where multiplicity comes from. At best, it seems like we should have a sequence of simple effects descending from God in a chain, each member of the chain causing one and only one additional member. As we know, Ibn Sīnā actually thought that something like this is true. There is a chain of immaterial intellects that descend from God, which are associated with the heavenly spheres. But where do these spheres, and their souls, come from? And how do we get the complex region down here where we live, where the four elements are combined into composite substances?

To explain this Ibn Sīnā again invokes modal properties. Whereas God is necessary, the first intellect to emanate forth from Him is contingent. But it is also caused to exist, indeed 'necessitated' by God to do so. So where God had only one thing to think about, namely Himself, the first intellect has *three* things to think about: God, itself as contingent, and itself as necessitated by God.

God's knowledge of particulars

Suppose that I get up in the morning and have toast for breakfast. Most Muslims, indeed most adherents of Abrahamic religions more generally, would assume that God knows I am having toast. Ibn Sīnā was an exception, or at least, he believed that God knows this in a surpassingly unusual way. To see why, we need to cast our minds back to the strict demands of the Aristotelian theory of knowledge further developed by Ibn Sīnā. Knowledge in the proper sense means grasping universal intelligible objects, this being the work of the intellect. Since God is an intellect, it seems obvious that this is the kind of knowledge He should have too. Now, humans are able to deploy their universal knowledge by applying it to particular cases. If I know universally that toast contains flour, then when I see toast on my plate I can know that *this* piece of toast contains flour. But that requires me to use a lower cognitive power, in this case vision, which acquaints me with *this* piece of toast.

Since God is a pure intellect it isn't clear how He could do this, that is, how He could become aware of particulars in order to subsume them under His universal, intellectual knowledge. Indeed, as Ibn Sīnā points out, there is good reason to suppose that God *cannot* have such direct awareness of particulars, since this would induce change in Him as He tracks the changing objects of that awareness. Instead, he proposes that God does know about particulars, but only universally, not *as particulars*. His example is that one could know about the occurrence of a particular eclipse as a kind of corollary of general knowledge about the heavenly motions. Why though would God have even this sort of general knowledge? Well, within Ibn Sīnā's deterministic system, all particular existents and events can be traced back to God. So it is only by knowing Himself as a cause that He can know about particulars being subsumed under universals. Unlike us, He has no direct acquaintance with them.

Ibn Sīnā must have known that this was a provocative thing to say. To forestall the objection that he was contradicting the teaching of the Quran, he took what was for him the rare step of quoting Scripture. His theory, he insisted, confirms that 'not even the weight of an atom in heaven or on earth is hidden from Him' (Quran 10:61). But many later authors were not convinced, and polemicized against this teaching as one of Ibn Sīnā's most flagrant departures from acceptable belief.

Happily, there are exactly three things it needs to generate in turn, namely the next intellect in the chain, its own heavenly sphere, and the soul that moves that sphere. So its three distinct intellectual acts give rise to three distinct effects. As for our lower world of elements, its complexity can now be explained through the motions of the spheres. These motions facilitate a transition from the eternal realm of the celestial bodies, where nothing is ever generated or destroyed, to our lower realm of more temporary beings. As we can see from the fact that plant growth and animal reproduction are correlated to the motions of the Sun, the variations in spatial location in the upper world lead to more extreme forms of change in the lower world.

Something I just said may worry you (perhaps several things, but let's focus on just one). I mentioned that the first intellect is 'necessitated' by God, because it cannot but come forth from Him. Furthermore, that necessitation carries on, since the first intellect *must* give rise to its three effects. But this means that the celestial intellects, souls, and spheres are necessarily existent! Wasn't that status reserved for God? Not quite. God is unique in being the only being that is 'necessary in itself' (*wājib bi-dhātihi*), since the divine essence is the only one that guarantees its own existence. The celestial entities, and the universe as a whole, are also necessary. But they are 'necessary through another' (*wājib bi-ghayrihi*), either through God directly in the case of the first intellect, or in all other cases through a chain of causes that goes back to God.

What about things in the lower world below the heavens? Is all contingency down here reduced to necessity once we consider the causal chain leading (now very indirectly) back to God? In other words, was Ibn Sīnā a determinist? The answer seems to be yes. There is a section of the logical part of *The Healing* that corresponds to Aristotle's *On Interpretation*, which itself has a famous discussion of determinism. In this context Ibn Sīnā remarks that 'everything is necessary, but it may be either necessary in itself, or necessary through the occurrence of a cause that renders it necessary'. Future events are an exception, but only in a sense. They have not *yet* been rendered necessary, but they will be once their causes arrive. The same goes for human actions. We do 'will' them, but are necessitated to do so by our desires, beliefs, and so on, in such a way that the actions will inevitably proceed so long as we have the power to perform them. And our desires, beliefs, and so on have their own causes, which necessitate them.

It was inevitable that Ibn Sīnā should be a determinist, and not just because according to determinism everything is inevitable. It follows from his analysis of contingency and causation. As he says in the *Book of Knowledge*, 'nothing is until it becomes necessary', and though we often do not know the causes of what has happened, is happening, or will happen, all these things are in fact necessitated at the moment of their occurrence. If one objected to him that one thing can cause another without making it necessary, he would simply disagree. To cause something just is to 'preponderate' it so that its possibility for both being and not being is decided in one direction or another. Until something is necessitated, its occurrence has not yet been explained; perhaps it has been made more likely, but it has not been *caused*. To put this in the language of today's philosophers, for Ibn Sīnā every genuine cause is a 'sufficient' cause, that is, a cause that guarantees that its effect follows. Subsequent philosophers in the Islamic world similarly spoke of a 'complete' cause. This might include not only the obvious cause of something, like fire for burning, but also those factors that prevent any impediment (heat shielding, say) that could stop the thing from being burnt.

As so often, it is worth pausing here to compare Ibn Sīnā's position to that of the *kalām* schools. In particular, the Ash'arites are well known for having espoused a form of 'occasionalism', according to which all things are caused by God, which sounds a little like Ibn Sīnā's view. There are a couple of significant differences between Ibn Sīnā and the Ash'arites. For one thing, they have God directly causing everything to happen, creating even human actions, whereas Ibn Sīnā's God is very 'hands off', with a direct causal relation only to the first celestial intellect. For another thing and more importantly, the Ash'arites do not believe that God's will in causing all these things to happen is itself necessary. For them, God is a voluntary (*mukhtār*) agent who is capable of making decisions that could have fallen otherwise. Al-Ghazālī memorably illustrates this idea with the example of a man allowed to take one of two equally appealing dates. The man can take either date, having no reason to prefer one over the other, so he simply chooses one arbitrarily. Similarly God can make arbitrary choices such as, say, the first moment at which the universe will exist.

Ibn Sīnā's universe is thus genuinely deterministic because necessity begins with God and flows downwards from there, whereas the Ash'arite universe is deterministic only in the sense that all things are subject to God's contingent will. This became the core of al-Ghazālī's opposition to Ibn Sīnā's philosophical theology. Seeing things from an Ash'arite point of view, al-Ghazālī said that Ibn Sīnā's God would not even be a proper 'agent' (*fā'il*), but more like an automatic or natural cause, like fire radiating heat without choosing to do so. The use of the Neoplatonic language of 'emanation' seems to confirm that impression. It suggests that God is like a shining light or overflowing fountain, not a voluntary agent. But Ibn Sīnā anticipates this line of criticism and answers it. He explicitly says that choice need not be between different open possibilities. What is required is instead an absence of external constraint—which is of course satisfied in God's case, since nothing else forces Him to cause the universe—and that the action in question proceeds from the cause's knowledge, power, and will. So as far as he is concerned, God is a voluntary agent, despite exerting His causation necessarily.

Good and evil

'Goodness' is another attribute that Ibn Sīnā derives from necessity. In fact God is according to him 'pure good' (*khayr maḥḍ*) and 'pure perfection' (*kamāl maḥḍ*), because goodness is for him correlated with existence and actuality, and as the necessary existent God has perfect existence and actuality. These statements too are reminiscent of the Neoplatonic tradition. The phrase 'pure good' appears even in the title of the Arabic translation of Proclus' *Elements of Theology* (in Arabic known as *Book of the Pure Good*, later in Latin as the *Book of Causes*), and the equation of being with goodness is familiar from Plotinus. Conversely, Plotinus put forward the very influential idea that evil is simply non-being or absence of perfection, a view also adopted by Ibn Sīnā. As he puts it in the *Salvation*, 'what suffers absence in any way is not entirely free of evil and deficiency'. For example, natural evils might include things like a body's failure to have a healthy balance of the four humours, while moral evils would involve a deficit of rationality or self-control.

It is easy to get confused here, since this theory of evil as privation is often referred to as a 'theodicy', suggesting that it is supposed to explain why God would allow evil. But it looks like a very unconvincing answer to that question, since we could just ask why

God allows there to be such absences rather than making everything in the world perfect, so that every human is virtuous, every body healthy, and so on. In fact, the privation theory was not designed to respond to what we usually call the 'problem of evil', but to show that evils are not *causally* traceable to the perfectly good first principle. Since evils are just absences, they are not existents that need to be produced by God, whether directly or through indirect causation. Rather they are yet another example of necessary concomitants: they arise only as inevitable, dependent consequences of the things that God did produce.

Ibn Sīnā has an entirely different answer to the problem of theodicy, that is, the question why God allows evils. It looks very much like the position taken in late antiquity by Proclus. The basic idea is that as the diverse things in our earthly realm pursue their diverse goods, they will so to speak 'get in each other's way'. Ibn Sīnā gives the example of a garment burned by fire. It is a 'great good' for the world that there is fire and that it is hot, by its very essence. But if the world contains fire, sometimes things are going to get burnt. This is a shame, but we shouldn't overreact to such phenomena. Ibn Sīnā stresses that in general, the good far outweighs the bad. If it were on balance a bad thing that fire existed, because so many garments were getting destroyed that this overwhelmed the benefits provided by fire, then God's providence would see to it that there is no fire. But of course that is not the case. Even when it comes to moral goodness, he adopts the refreshingly optimistic view that although truly virtuous humans are rare, so are extremely vicious humans. The vast majority lie somewhere in between, and are good enough that they will be rewarded rather than punished in the afterlife.

Nor is this just a matter of good luck. As we saw earlier (Chapter 2), Ibn Sīnā believed that the gifts of divine providence include the sending of prophets to lay down laws that will lead people to an orderly society and good afterlife. His views on ethics, as presented for example towards the end of the metaphysics in

The Healing and in a short work entitled *On the Science of Ethics* (*Fī ʿIlm al-Akhlāq*), are uncharacteristically conventional. He affirms Aristotle's definition of virtues and vices as character traits that arise through habituation, with virtues lying in the mean between extremes. Also endorsed are familiar Platonic doctrines like the tripartite soul (reason, spirit, desire) and the need for the soul to turn away from the concerns of the body.

More distinctive, though prefigured in al-Fārābī, is his integration of these familiar ethical concepts with the lawgiving role of the prophet-ruler, which is further set within the context of the whole cosmic order. The lawgiver sees to it that the community fulfils religious obligations, like prayer, and institutes practices that are conducive to social stability, like marriage with the possibility of divorce. As so often, Ibn Sīnā approaches these matters in a self-consciously philosophical way while also speaking to a broader audience. In this case he is offering a systematic rationale for Islamic jurisprudence, whose role is to study exactly the laws laid down for the aforementioned purposes. As this chapter has shown, Ibn Sīnā was not afraid to make provocative claims, which he surely knew would elicit objections from mainstream intellectuals. But equally, he offered those intellectuals many opportunities to appreciate the relevance of his philosophy. And appreciate it they did.

Chapter 6
Ibn Sīnā's legacy

From the Iberian Peninsula and the British Isles in the west to central Asia in the east, no philosopher of the medieval era had an influence comparable to that of Ibn Sīnā. This is simply because no other figure spanned cultural divides as he did. Directly or indirectly, he shaped philosophy in the Islamic world for a full millennium after his death. He was massively influential in European Christendom too, in this case for about half a millennium, stretching from the first Latin translations of his works in the 12th century down to the early modern period, when he remained a major figure in medical literature and still relevant for thinkers like Descartes, Leibniz, and Spinoza. In contrast to his stature among Muslim and Christian intellectuals, Jewish thinkers did not embrace him as a major figure. But even here his ideas circulated, if often indirectly. In the *Kuzari* of Judah Hallevi (d. 1141), a dialogue in which a king chooses between the belief systems of Judaism, Christianity, Islam, and 'philosophy', the last option is strikingly close to a summary of Ibn Sīnā's philosophy. This is an echo of the way that Ibn Sīnā had come to define *falsafa* in the Islamic world. Of course Hallevi does not recommend *falsafa* as the correct set of teachings, and that too is not atypical. Ibn Sīnā was just as important in provoking opposition as in winning adherents.

5. Tomb of Ibn Sīnā in Hamadhān, Iran.

The Islamic world

To tell the full story of Ibn Sīnā's reception in the Islamic world would be too large a task for the present context, so I will focus here on the few centuries immediately following his death. His ideas were immediately taken up by a small number of students and associates, whose works are sometimes little more than patchworks of quotation from the master's texts. Among these figures the most significant historically seems to have been Bahmanyār (d. 1044). His philosophical exchanges with Ibn Sīnā are recorded in the *Discussions* (*Mubāḥathāt*), and he wrote a systematic survey of Ibn Sīnā's philosophy that seems to have been read widely as a useful and authoritative presentation of that philosophy.

Where Bahmanyār was a faithful disciple, a series of other thinkers challenged Ibn Sīnā, often approaching him from a *kalām* perspective. This is true of the Ashʿarite al-Ghazālī

6. Iranian postage stamp of Ibn Sīnā.

(d. 1111), who has been mentioned several times already as the author of the famous *Incoherence of the Philosophers*, and the Muʿtazilite Ibn al-Malāḥimī (d. 1141). His *Gift for the Scholars of Kalām* (*Tuḥfat al-mutakallimīn*) updates traditional Muʿtazilism for a post-Ibn Sīnā world, defending the teachings of his own school against both Ashʿarism and *falsafa*. Around the same time Tāj al-Dīn al-Shahrastāni (d. 1153) undertook a related project, which set a template for philosophy in succeeding generations. His *Utmost Point of Progress in the Science of Kalām* (*Nihāyat al-aqdām fī ʿilm al-kalām*) compares Ashʿarism, Muʿtazilism, and *falsafa*, where the latter means specifically the philosophy of Ibn Sīnā. Here we can see that Ibn Sīnā's thought has become one among a small number of systems worth taking seriously for the Islamic mainstream. In the Islamic East, he has supplanted Aristotle as the figure who most embodies *falsafa*. Around this period, the one real exception in the East was ʿAbd al-Lāṭif al-Baġdādī (d. 1231), whose animus towards Ibn Sīnā led him to comment pointedly on Aristotle, as if that were still a relevant thing to do.

A parallel, and much more successful, attempt to do the same thing was undertaken by Ibn Rushd (in Latin, Averroes, d. 1198) in Muslim Spain. He devoted huge effort to expounding the works of Aristotle, using several formats: epitomes, running paraphrases, and, for a handful of important works, full-dress commentaries that quote Aristotle in Arabic translation and then discuss the quotations at length. But even Ibn Rushd was not immune to the impact of Ibn Sīnā. He critiqued the latter on numerous points, both small and large. For instance, in psychology he dispensed with Ibn Sīnā's faculty of *wahm*, while in metaphysics he rejected the famous proof of God's existence on methodological grounds. In his opinion, metaphysics has God as part of its subject matter, and no science should prove the existence of its own subjects. Instead, Ibn Rushd followed Aristotle by establishing God's existence within natural philosophy, as the prime cause of motion in the cosmos. It is then up to the metaphysician to explore more fully God's nature and His relationship to the cosmos.

Ibn Rushd was effectively trying to undo the damage done by the arrival of Ibn Sīnā, which was for him demonstrated by al-Ghazālī's *Incoherence*. In his *Incoherence of the Incoherence*, Ibn Rushd took umbrage at al-Ghazālī's attacking philosophy, and especially at the unspoken assumption that *falsafa* meant Ibn Sīnā, not Aristotle. Repeatedly, he dismissed al-Ghazālī's critiques as irrelevant, because they were aimed at positions not to be found in Aristotle. Ibn Rushd partially prevailed in his rear-guard action. Especially in the Jewish tradition, his influence came to dwarf Ibn Sīnā's, because his commentaries on Aristotle were rendered into Hebrew. As we'll see below, he also rivalled and sometimes exceeded Ibn Sīnā as the most impactful Muslim philosopher in the Latin scholastic context. But we should not jump to the conclusion that Ibn Sīnā was relevant in the far Islamic West only as a foil for an Aristotelian resurgence. Ibn Rushd's associate Ibn Ṭufayl (d. 1185) wrote *Ḥayy Ibn Yaqẓān*, a kind of philosophical novel in which a man grows up isolated on an island and independently becomes a fully accomplished philosopher and mystic. As is clear from both the prologue to *Ḥayy* and the arguments unfolded in the work, Ibn Ṭufayl had imperfect access to Ibn Sīnā's philosophy but still made good use of it. Indeed the premise of the story is that the main character Ḥayy is spontaneously generated from the earth, a possibility that Ibn Sīnā had notoriously allowed.

It is sometimes said that Ibn Rushd had almost no legacy in the pre-modern Islamic world, precisely because his ambition of putting Aristotle back at the core of philosophical discussion was outmoded. While this is not entirely the case, it is true that among his co-religionists Ibn Rushd was a mere footnote in comparison to Ibn Sīnā. If we turn now back to the Islamic East, we find that in the period running up to and through the time of the Mongol invasions in the middle of the 13th century, philosophy was flourishing and was primarily an engagement with Ibn Sīnā's ideas. One could mention literally dozens of thinkers here, who run the gamut from outraged critics—for instance Šarāf al-Dīn al-Mas'ūdī (d. *c.*1194), author of a relentlessly critical response to the *Pointers*—to staunch defenders like Naṣīr al-Dīn al-Ṭūsī (d. 1274). He is rightly famous as an astronomer but also wrote a commentary of his own on the *Pointers*, which defended that work against the critiques of Fakhr al-Dīn al-Rāzī (see Chapter 1).

Fakhr al-Dīn (d. 1210) was one of three roughly contemporaneous thinkers who all attempted to do to Ibn Sīnā what he had managed to do to Aristotle. That is, they presented themselves as systematic and synoptic thinkers of such genius that they could survey the whole intellectual terrain of their times and stand in judgement over it all, while adding novel ideas and arguments of their own. The ambition is sometimes clear even from the titles of their works. Just as Ibn Sīnā wrote *The Fair Judgement*, so the Jewish–Muslim convert Abū l-Barakāt al-Baghdādī (d. 1165) produced *The Carefully Considered* (*al-Muʿtabar*). We've seen a good example of his approach already, with his 'careful consideration' and rejection of Ibn Sīnā's faculty psychology (see Chapter 3). On this point and some others he was followed by Fakhr al-Dīn, who in recent research is emerging as perhaps the most exciting and philosophically acute of the thinkers in this period.

He has some competition for that honour from a third major figure of the time, Shihāb al-Dīn al-Suhrawardī (d. 1191). Actually he is the most famous of the three, thanks in part to his having been put to death on the orders of Saladin, and in part to his having developed a new and idiosyncratic approach to philosophy called 'Illuminationism'. Or one might better say, for claiming to have done this. Close inspection of his full range of works shows that, far from abandoning Ibn Sīnā for an entirely new philosophy based around the concept of light, al-Suhrawardī was in fact closely engaged with Ibn Sīnā (and *kalām*) in much the same way as his contemporaries, often reaching similar conclusions. His most widely read work, the *Philosophy of Illumination* (*Ḥikmat al-ishrāq*), does frame his ideas in the way promised by its title. God is a 'first Light' from whom derive other lights, which play the role of Ibn Sīnā's celestial intellects but are far more numerous. Furthermore, al-Suhrawardī held a number of views that were diametrically opposed to Ibn Sīnā's, for instance his rejection of the possibility of providing real definitions, and his positing of Platonic Forms. But he always articulated his own views through critique of Ibn Sīnā, much as Abū l-Barakāt and Fakhr al-Dīn were doing around the same time. If Suhrawardī looms larger in modern secondary literature, this is mostly because his philosophy was taken up in early modern Iran during the Safavid era, especially by the towering figure Mullā Ṣadrā. Ṣadrā (d. 1640) remains central in Iranian philosophy to this day and was himself a conduit for the influence of Ibn Sīnā.

Mullā Ṣadrā

The 17th-century philosopher Ṣadr al-Dīn al-Shīrāzī, commonly known as Mullā Ṣadrā, was not the terminus of the tradition of thought initiated by Ibn Sīnā, but he was certainly one of its greatest exponents. He benefited from a resurgence of interest in the Greek–Arabic translations produced in the formative phase of philosophy in the Islamic world, like the *Theology of Aristotle*. Ṣadrā was a syncretic thinker who knew his Ibn Sīnā but also drew heavily on Suhrawardī's Illuminationism and on the mysticism of the great philosophical Sufi, Ibn ʿArabī (d. 1240). Ṣadrā's signature doctrine can be traced back directly to Ibn Sīnā, though it is refracted through the lens of Sufism. From this tradition he adopted the doctrine of the 'unity of existence' (*waḥdat al-wujūd*): all existence is ultimately divine, and things other than God are mere appearances or manifestations of this single being. Mystical insight is duly understood as an awareness of one's own unity with existence. Ṣadrā took this idea and combined it with one explored elsewhere in this chapter, the 'modulation (*tashkīk*) of existence'. For him the difference between God and other things is a contrast between pure, unmodulated existence and lesser, diminished forms of existence that remain grounded in God for their reality. Suhrawardī offered him the perfect language for expressing this idea: God is a pure light and other things are arranged beneath him in a series of ever dimmer lights. No wonder that Ṣadrā appreciated the *Theology of Aristotle*, since his own vision was remarkably similar to the hierarchical metaphysics of Neoplatonism.

Definitions, existence, eternity

So much for the personalities. What were the ideas of Ibn Sīnā that had the most purchase in this context? Well, practically all of them. But let's take a few representative examples, which I'll draw from three different areas of Ibn Sīnā's thought: logic, metaphysics, and cosmology. Logic was an area where great innovations emerged within Ibn Sīnā's system, especially at the hands of al-Khūnajī (d. 1248). Another important figure here, not least for his widely disseminated textbook on logic, *Epistle for Shams al-Dīn* (*Risāla al-Shamsiyya*), was al-Kātibī al-Qazwīnī (d. 1276). Since their contributions are often quite technical, though, I'll focus here on a more easily explained issue: a sceptical stance towards definitions.

As we saw in Chapter 2, definitions play a crucial role in Ibn Sīnā's logic. By capturing our conceptualizations, they provide the starting point for syllogistic demonstration. Now, exploiting Ibn Sīnā's link between definition and conceptualization, Abū l-Barakāt, al-Suhrawardī, and al-Rāzī all argued that the process of 'making something known' (*ta'rīf*) can really only ever convey how a given person is understanding a term. Of course there can be more and less adequate understandings, better and worse perspectives on things. But you cannot argue with someone's definition: it just expresses their conceptualization, and a conceptualization is just a way of thinking about something. Thus all definitions are bound to be merely *nominal*. As we saw, nominal definitions pick something out under a certain description, but do not necessarily reveal the essence or 'true nature' of that thing. The upshot is that we cannot advance our knowledge just by articulating a definition. Rather the definition merely expresses what one has already learned, through sense-perception or some other form of direct acquaintance.

This is typical of philosophy in the Islamic East after Ibn Sīnā, in that reflection on his epistemology often led in a rather sceptical direction. One worry was that reason itself may be subject to doubt. Al-Ghazālī notoriously said in his autobiography *The Deliverer from Error* (*Munqidh min al-Dalāl*) that he was able to fend off a sceptical crisis along these lines only thanks to God, who gave him certain confidence in the dictates of his own intellect.

A worry more closely related to Ibn Sīnā's thought was provoked by the high bar he set for knowledge. His standard for knowledge in the strict and proper sense, that it is established by valid syllogisms grounded ultimately in certain first principles, was bound to provoke the thought that we rarely if ever achieve this. Several modern-day scholars have suggested that this concern prompted a characteristically 'dialectical' form of writing in the 12th to 13th centuries. Arguments and counter-arguments, and counter-counter-arguments, and so on, were weighed up on all sides of every issue, often with only tentative conclusions about where this survey of considerations should leave us. A good example is Fakhr al-Dīn, who tended to indicate only a balance of probability on a given question and finish with the remark, 'but God knows best!' Where he was more confident in a conclusion, it was usually because he took himself to have ruled out rival views, not because he was able to offer positive, ironclad proofs for that conclusion.

Ibn Sīnā's metaphysics provided another nudge in a sceptical direction by introducing the notion of mental existence. Much as one might worry that conceptualizations do not fully latch on to real essences, so one might worry that a given essence is in fact realized only in the mind, not in concrete reality. Things are pretty clear with centaurs and giraffes: the former exist only mentally, the latter concretely. But what about a phenomenon like time? In a typical illustration of his dialectical style, Fakhr al-Dīn offered a long discussion of whether time exists and considered at length not one but two possible sceptical positions about it. First that time does not exist at all, because it is an inherently contradictory notion, and thus impossible in itself. Second that time does exist, but only in the mind; that is, it is a purely subjective phenomenon. In the end he argued that time does exist in reality. Still, his procedure suggested that the burden of proof lay on the realist.

Existence was more generally one of the topics of Ibn Sīnā's philosophy that provoked the most debate, in part because his own position was rather unclear. As the later philosophers saw, there was a dilemma at the heart of his metaphysics. On the one hand he drew a contrast between the necessary being, who has existence through Himself, and contingent beings, which have existence through a cause. This seems to imply that existence is the same for both God and other things. They would differ only in their way of having existence: God intrinsically, other things extrinsically. So on this view 'existence' is *univocal*, that is, it always means the same thing. On the other hand, Ibn Sīnā sometimes seemed to suggest that the divine essence *just is* pure existence, so as to safeguard God's simplicity. If this is true, then God's existence is clearly very different from mine or yours, since my existence or yours is presumably not identical with God (though philosophical mystics like Mullā Ṣadrā thought otherwise). That impression was apparently confirmed when Ibn Sīnā, especially in some late works, spoke of *tashkīk*, meaning 'modulation' or 'analogy'. The idea would be that the existence of contingent beings is a different and lesser version of the existence that belongs to God, or just is God. This then would be an *analogical* theory of existence.

We duly find a healthy debate in the later period over whether existence is one and the same phenomenon for all existents, or different in different cases. The main partisan of the univocity view was Fakhr al-Dīn al-Rāzī, who suggested that metaphysics is the study of a unified concept of existence, which is then sub-divided into necessary and contingent, eternal and non-eternal, one or many, actual or potential, and so on (he gave no fewer than 20 such disjunctive pairings). He presented several arguments for univocity, for instance that *non*-existence is always the same idea. So its converse, existence, should also always be the same. Furthermore, one can doubt whether something exists without conceptualizing it as necessary or contingent. So the doubt must concern a univocal notion of existence that applies to both the necessary and the contingent. Partisans of the analogical theory of existence, like al-Ṭūsī, refuted these arguments. They also observed that we don't even need to get into the difficult case of God to see that existence means different things in different cases, because an accident doesn't exist in the same sense as the substance to which it belongs. My baldness is a dependent entity, whereas I am a self-subsisting one, thus my baldness and I do not 'exist' in precisely the same sense.

Another debate concerned the very contrast between existence and essence. Are they distinguished in the real concrete world, or only in our mental conceptions? Al-Suhrawardī was prominent, though far from unusual, in adopting a *conceptualist* position on existence. He and others contended that absurdities would arise if we were to postulate extramental existence. A common argument here was that if extramental essences need to receive existence in order to be concretely realized, then the same should go for extramental existence. Thus when a giraffe exists, the existence of the giraffe would also need to exist. But this second-order existence would also need to exist, and so on, yielding an absurd infinite regress.

Let us turn now to Ibn Sīnā's cosmology, and in particular his commitment to the eternity of the universe. This was one of his most hotly contested teachings, along with his positions on the afterlife and God's knowledge. His eternalism seemed to deny the clear meaning of the Quran and its praise of God as Creator of all things. Of course Ibn Sīnā would say that God does 'create' all things in the sense of being their ultimate cause. In fact he held that a real cause exists whenever its effect does, because the effect keeps depending on it for its continued existence. So for him causation, including divine creation, need not involve initiating the existence of something. It is about maintaining a thing's existence, for the whole time of its existence—which may be an eternal time. By contrast, in *kalām* it was typically assumed that to create something means bringing something to exist at a certain moment, *after* it was non-existent.

This is why al-Ghazālī devoted so much attention to the issue in his *Incoherence of the Philosophers*. For him asserting the eternity of the universe, as Ibn Sīnā had done, meant refusing to acknowledge God as the almighty Creator praised in the Quran. In thinkers after al-Ghazālī we find even longer treatments of the issue, over many dozens or even hundreds of pages. Detailed attention was paid to such questions as whether God can decide to create something but then 'delay' doing so, such that His will would be eternal but have a non-eternal effect; non-temporal senses in which God could be 'prior' to the universe; whether it is possible that an infinity of events, for instance revolutions of the celestial spheres, can already have elapsed prior to now; and whether the possibility of the universe's existence needs to be grounded in matter, so that matter at least must be eternal. At the heart of this debate lies the contrast already noted in the last chapter, Ibn Sīnā's necessitarian God as opposed to the voluntarist God of *kalām*. The eternity of the universe was not debated only for its own sake, but as an occasion to settle the issue between those two positions.

Latin Christendom

The eternity of the universe was no less a matter of contention in the Latin West, but there the debate centred on Aristotle rather than 'Avicenna'. On the whole it cannot be disputed that medieval Latin scholasticism treated Aristotle as the main authority within philosophy. In fact he was often just called 'the Philosopher', while Ibn Rushd or 'Averroes' was 'the Commentator', the most authoritative guide to Aristotle's thought. But this did not preclude Ibn Sīnā from playing a major role. At first his influence could even exceed that of Aristotle, because his works were translated so early.

In Toledo and then in Burgos, speakers of Arabic (often Jews) were available to collaborate with Christians to usher philosophical texts from the Islamic world into Latin. Parts of Ibn

Sīnā's *The Healing* got this treatment in the second half of the 12th century, in part thanks to a translator named 'Avendauth', probably to be identified with the Jewish philosopher Abraham Ibn Daud (d. *c.*1180). In one of the great ironies of medieval philosophy, al-Ghazālī ('Algazel') was taken to be a further source for understanding Ibn Sīnā's ideas, rather than as his greatest critic. This is because al-Ghazālī had written the *Intentions of the Philosophers* (*Maqāṣid al-falāsifa*), a summary of the philosophy of Ibn Sīnā, as preparatory background for its demolition in the *Incoherence*. On the basis of the Latin version of the *Intentions*, al-Ghazālī was taken to be a disciple of Ibn Sīnā. Albert the Great (d. 1280) even referred to 'Algazel, who follows [Avicenna] in everything' (*qui eum in omnibus sequitur*).

It was only around the time of Albert the Great and his disciple Thomas Aquinas (d. 1274) that Ibn Rushd emerged as the most important guide to Aristotle, and thus the most widely consulted thinker of the Islamic world. Prior to that we find scholastics of the first half of the 13th century, like William of Auvergne (d. 1249), drawing on Ibn Sīnā to understand Aristotle's *Metaphysics* and for theorizing about the soul. At this time and still later, the flying man thought experiment was on the list of standard arguments for the incorporeality of the soul. Ibn Sīnā's proof from the nature of intellection, that a universal cannot be received in a bodily organ, was also known. In fact it was still being cited in the high Renaissance by Marsilio Ficino (d. 1499), who called it 'an argument of the Arabic Platonists' (*Platonicorum Arabum sententia*).

Other aspects of Ibn Sīnā's psychology also had a long afterlife, such as his theory of the Active Intellect as 'giver of forms' (*dator formarum*). William of Auvergne even ascribed it to Aristotle, so convinced was he that Ibn Sīnā was a reliable guide to philosophical tradition. Ibn Sīnā's controversial claim that the Active Intellect could cause even a human to be spontaneously generated was discussed well into the Renaissance, and routinely connected to the name of 'Avicenna'. Also pervasive was knowledge about *wahm* or *aestimatio*. Dag Nikolaus Hasse, in a study of the Latin reception of Ibn Sīnā's psychology, has observed that 'almost every writer after 1200 who wrote on the soul mentioned at least the basic ingredients of Avicenna's doctrine: the name of the faculty, the connotational attributes and the example of the sheep and the wolf'. Readers of Latin could draw on several sources for the doctrine: *The Healing* of course, but also al-Ghazālī's *Intentions*, and Ibn Sīnā's *Canon of Medicine*, which was widely read in both the medieval and Renaissance periods.

'Avicenna' as 'prince of physicians'

Ibn Sīnā's legacy in Christendom was not restricted to his philosophical influence. He was recognized as a great authority in medicine, the most important such authority from the Islamic world alongside Abū Bakr al-Rāzī; only Hippocrates and Galen were considered more important. Ibn Sīnā's status as 'prince of physicians' was due especially to the Latin translation of his *Canon*, though other medical treatises of his were also translated. Here as in the Islamic world the *Canon* was recognized as an invaluable overview of the whole of medicine. Ibn Sīnā's works were on the curriculum at faculties of medicine around Europe, not least in Bologna, the leading university for this discipline. During the Renaissance, some argued in keeping with the values of the humanist movement that the medicine of 'the Arabs' (never mind that al-Rāzī and Ibn Sīnā were Persians) should be discarded, for the sake of getting back to the truer wisdom of the original Greeks. This sentiment paralleled what we find in philosophy, where scholasticism and its Arabic sources were rejected by the humanists.

Yet the sheer usefulness of Ibn Sīnā made it difficult to dispense with him. A study of Latin editions of the *Canon* has counted at least 60 between 1500 and 1674, and it was also made the basis of commentaries and new translations. The anatomist Berengario di Carpi (d. 1530) quoted Ibn Sīnā more than 1,000 times; this compared to only about 600 citations of Aristotle. Even such a self-consciously humanistic doctor as Symphorien Champier (d. 1538) expressed his disdain for would-be experts who had 'never read Galen and Avicenna'. Another French doctor of the same century, Jean Fernel (d. 1588), was not guilty of this charge. He discussed Ibn Sīnā's example of scammony in a work devoted to the rather 'Avicennan' idea that there are underlying causes in things that cannot be discovered directly by sensation. On the whole, Ibn Sīnā's reception as a medical author was no less significant than his reception as a philosopher, something well captured by none other than Dante Alighieri, who in the fourth *canto* of *Inferno* puts Ibn Sīnā in limbo, right next to Hippocrates and Galen.

Still, it may have been as a philosopher of existence that Ibn Sīnā had his most far-reaching influence in Christendom. A debate over existence in the late 13th century, which is one of the most famous episodes of Latin medieval philosophy, was actually an unwitting reprise of the controversy that had unfolded about a century earlier in the Islamic East. The 'analogy' theory of existence was paralleled by Aquinas' understanding of being. He accepted a distinction between being and essence, even writing a work called *De Ente et Essentia*, and argued that this distinction breaks down in the one case of God. For God is identical with existence, or is 'being itself' (*esse ipsum*). Now, it should be said that Aquinas did not take himself to be simply reiterating Ibn Sīnā's version of the essence–existence distinction. In part thanks to the way the translators had rendered the original Arabic texts, the Latin scholastics understood Ibn Sīnā to be saying that existence is 'accidental' to essence. This looks like an unconvincing claim, because it would suggest that essence already 'is something' before it receives existence. We would be back, by a circuitous route, to the Muʿtazilite thesis that something non-existent may be a real thing. In fact, though, Ibn Sīnā said that existence is 'concomitant' (*lāzim*) to essence. This may or may not have exactly the same meaning as we discussed while looking at his logic, but it at least means that essence and existence are inseparable. So, had Aquinas been able to read Ibn Sīnā in Arabic, perhaps he would have been more prepared to see himself as an 'Avicennan', especially if he had also been given access to the works of later partisans of the analogy interpretation, like al-Ṭūsī.

As for the univocity view, in the Latin context this was defended by, among others, Henry of Ghent (d. 1294) and Duns Scotus (d. 1308). Scotus even proposed that existence is a unified general notion that is then divided by a series of dichotomies, exactly as Fakhr al-Dīn al-Rāzī had argued. This looks like an astounding coincidence, until you notice that al-Rāzī himself said he was simply expanding on a point already made by Ibn Sīnā. He and Scotus expressed similar theories of existence because they were both drawing on the same source. This is just one example of the way that two distinct 'scholastic' traditions, one in Arabic and Persian, the other in Latin, drew on the rich resources provided by Ibn Sīnā's philosophy. Few thinkers in world history have had such a long-lasting and philosophically fruitful legacy. In light of the personality so vividly on show in the *Autobiography*, I doubt that this would have surprised Ibn Sīnā himself.

Further reading

Here I provide suggestions organized by the topics of the chapters in this book. I have restricted myself to English language publications, but it should be borne in mind that there is important secondary literature on Ibn Sīnā in many languages, especially Arabic, French, German, Italian, and Persian.

For extensive further bibliography see J. Janssens, *An Annotated Bibliography on Ibn Sīnā* (Leuven: Leuven University Press, 1991); supplement published 1999.

General studies

P. Adamson (ed.), *Interpreting Avicenna: Critical Essays* (Cambridge: Cambridge University Press, 2013).

J. McGinnis, *Avicenna* (New York: Oxford University Press, 2010).

D. C. Reisman (ed.), *Before and After Avicenna* (Leiden: Brill, 2003).

R. Wisnovsky (ed.), *Aspects of Avicenna* (Princeton: Markus Wiener, 2001).

There are also several useful pages on aspects of Ibn Sīnā's thought on the online Stanford Enyclopedia of Philosophy: <plato. stanford.edu>.

Chapter 1: Life and works

A. Bertolacci, *The Reception of Aristotle's Metaphysics in Avicenna's Kitāb al-Šifā'* (Leiden: Brill, 2006).

W. Gohlman (trans.), *The Life of Ibn Sina* (Albany, NY: SUNY Press, 1974).

D. Gutas, *Avicenna and the Aristotelian Tradition*, 2nd edition (Leiden: Brill, 2014).
D. C. Reisman, *The Making of the Avicennan Tradition: the Transmission, Contents, and Structure of Ibn Sīnā's al-Mubāḥaṯāt (the Discussions)* (Leiden: Brill, 2002).

Chapter 2: Logic and knowledge

S. Chatti, 'Avicenna on Possibility and Necessity', *History and Philosophy of Logic* 35 (2014), 332–53.
N. Rescher, *The Development of Arabic Logic* (Pittsburgh: University of Pittsburgh Press, 1964).
T. Street, 'An Outline of Avicenna's Syllogistic', *Archiv für Geschichte der Philosophie* 84 (2002), 129–60.
R. Strobino, *Avicenna's Theory of Science: Logic, Metaphysics, Epistemology* (Oakland, Calif.: University of California Press, 2021).

Chapter 3: The human person

P. Adamson and F. Benevich, 'The Thought Experimental Method: Avicenna's Flying Man Argument', *Journal of the American Philosophical Association* 4 (2018), 1–18.
T. Alpina, *Subject, Definition, Activity: Framing Avicenna's Science of the Soul* (Berlin: de Gruyter, 2021).
D. L. Black, 'Estimation in Avicenna: The Logical and Psychological Dimensions', *Dialogue* 32 (1993), 219–58.
D. L. Black, 'Avicenna on Self-Awareness and Knowing that One Knows', in S. Rahman et al. (eds), *The Unity of Science in the Arabic Tradition* (Dordrecht: Kluwer, 2008), 63–87.
T.-A. Druart, 'The Human Soul's Individuation and its Survival After the Body's Death: Avicenna on the Causal Relation Between Body and Soul', *Arabic Sciences and Philosophy* 10 (2000), 259–73.
S. Ogden, 'Avicenna's Emanated Abstraction', *Philosophers' Imprint* 20 (2020), 1–26.

Chapter 4: Science

D. Gutas, 'Medical Theory and Scientific Method in the Age of Avicenna', in D. C. Reisman (ed.), *Before and After Avicenna* (Leiden: Brill, 2003), 145–62.

J. Janssens, 'Experience (*Tajriba*) in Classical Arabic Philosophy (al-Fārābī-Avicenna)', *Quaestio* 4 (2004), 45–62.
A. Lammer, *The Elements of Avicenna's Physics: Greek Sources and Arabic Innovations* (Berlin: de Gruyter, 2018).
J. McGinnis, 'Avicenna's Naturalized Epistemology and Scientific Method', in S. Rahman, T. Street, and T. Hassan (eds), *The Unity of Science in the Arabic Tradition* (Dordrecht: Kluwer, 2008), 129–52.
P. E. Pormann, 'Avicenna on Medical Practice, Epistemology, and the Physiology of the Inner Senses', in P. Adamson (ed.), *Interpreting Avicenna: Critical Essays* (Cambridge: Cambridge University Press, 2013), 91–108.

Chapter 5: God and the world

P. Adamson, 'On Knowledge of Particulars', *Proceedings of the Aristotelian Society* 105 (2005), 273–94.
F. Benevich, 'God's Knowledge of Particulars: Avicenna, *Kalām*, and the Post-Avicennian Synthesis', *Recherches de théologie et philosophie médiévales* 76 (2019), 1–47.
A. Bertolacci, 'Avicenna and Averroes on the Proof of God's Existence and the Subject-Matter of Metaphysics', *Medioevo* 32 (2007), 61–98.
D. L. Black, 'Mental Existence in Thomas Aquinas and Avicenna', *Mediaeval Studies* 61 (1999), 45–79.
T.-A. Druart, '*Shay'* or *Res* as Concomitant of "Being" in Avicenna', *Documenti e Studi sulla Tradizione Filsofica Medievale* 12 (2001), 125–42.
O. Lizzini, '*Wujūd-Mawjūd*/Existence-Existent in Avicenna: A Key Ontological Notion of Arabic Philosophy', *Quaestio* 3 (2003), 11–38.
M. E. Marmura, 'Avicenna's Proof from Contingency for God's Existence in the *Metaphysics* of the *Shifā'*', *Medieval Studies* 42 (1980), 337–52.
T. Mayer, 'Avicenna's *Burhān al-Ṣiddiqīn*', *Journal of Islamic Studies* 12 (2001), 18–39.
R. Wisnovsky, 'Notes on Avicenna's Concept of Thingness (*shay'iyya*)', *Arabic Sciences and Philosophy* 10 (2000), 181–221.

Chapter 6: Ibn Sīnā's legacy

F. Benevich, 'The Essence–Existence Distinction: Four Elements of the Post-Avicennian Metaphysical Dispute (11–13th centuries)', *Oriens* 45 (2017), 1–52.

H. Eichner, '"Knowledge by Presence": Apperception and the Mind–Body Relationship. Fakhr al-Dīn al-Rāzī and al-Suhrawardī as Representatives of a Thirteenth Century Discussion', in P. Adamson (ed.), *In the Age of Averroes: Arabic Philosophy in the Sixth/Twelfth Century* (London: Warburg Institute, 2011), 117–40.

K. El-Rouayheb, 'Arabic Logic after Avicenna', in C. Dutilh Novaes and S. Read (eds), *The Cambridge Companion to Medieval Logic* (Cambridge: Cambridge University Press, 2016), 67–93.

F. Griffel, *The Formation of Post-Classical Philosophy in Islam* (Oxford: Oxford University Press, 2021).

D. N. Hasse, *Avicenna's De Anima in the Latin West* (London: Warburg Institute, 2000).

D. N. Hasse and A. Bertolacci (eds), *The Arabic, Hebrew and Latin Reception of Avicenna's Metaphysics* (Berlin: de Gruyter, 2011).

D. N. Hasse and A. Bertolacci (eds), *The Arabic, Hebrew and Latin Reception of Avicenna's Physics and Cosmology* (Berlin: de Gruyter, 2018).

D. Jacquart, 'The Influence of Arabic Medicine in the Medieval West', in R. Rashed (ed.), *Encyclopedia of the History of Arabic Science* (London: Routledge, 1996), vol. 3, 963–84.

J. L. Janssens and D. De Smet (eds), *Avicenna and His Heritage* (Leuven: Leuven University Press, 2002).

J. Kaukua, *Self-Awareness in Islamic Philosophy: Avicenna and Beyond* (Cambridge: Cambridge University Press, 2015).

Y. T. Langermann (ed.), *Avicenna and His Legacy: A Golden Age of Science and Philosophy* (Turnhout: Brepols, 2009).

A. Shihadeh, 'From al-Ghazālī to al-Rāzī: 6th/12th Century Developments in Muslim Philosophical Theology', *Arabic Sciences and Philosophy* 15 (2005), 141–79.

N. G. Siraisi, *Avicenna in Renaissance Italy* (Princeton: Princeton University Press, 1987).

R. Wisnovsky, 'One Aspect of the Avicennan Turn in Sunnī Theology', *Arabic Sciences and Philosophy* 14 (2004), 65–100.

Index

For the benefit of digital users, indexed terms that span two pages (e.g., 52–53) may, on occasion, appear on only one of those pages.

A

B

C

D

E

F

G

H

I

J

K

M

O

P

ISLAMIC HISTORY

A Very Short Introduction

Adam J. Silverstein

Does history matter? This book argues not that history matters, but that Islamic history does. This *Very Short Introduction* introduces the story of Islamic history; the controversies surrounding its study; and the significance that it holds - for Muslims and for non-Muslims alike. Opening with a lucid overview of the rise and spread of Islam, from the seventh to twenty first century, the book charts the evolution of what was originally a small, localised community of believers into an international religion with over a billion adherents. Chapters are also dedicated to the peoples - Arabs, Persians, and Turks - who shaped Islamic history, and to three representative institutions - the mosque, jihad, and the caliphate - that highlight Islam's diversity over time.

> 'The book is extremely lucid, readable, sensibly organised, and wears its considerable learning, as they say, 'lightly'.'
>
> BBC History Magazine

www.oup.com/vsi